T0300140

Innovative Change Management (ICM)

The **Management Handbooks for Results** Series

Innovative Change Management (ICM)
Preparing Your Organization for the New Innovative Culture

H. James Harrington

CRC Press
Taylor & Francis Group
Boca Raton London New York

CRC Press is an imprint of the
Taylor & Francis Group, an **informa** business

CRC Press
Taylor & Francis Group
6000 Broken Sound Parkway NW, Suite 300
Boca Raton, FL 33487-2742

International Standard Book Number-13: 978-0-8153-7078-9 (Hardback)
International Standard Book Number-13: 978-1-351-24855-6 (eBook)

Library of Congress Cataloging-in-Publication Data

Names: Harrington, H. J. (H. James), author.
Title: Innovative change management (ICM) : preparing your organization for the new innovative culture / H. James Harrington.
Description: Boca Raton, FL : CRC Press, 2018. | Series: Management handbooks for results | Includes index.
Identifiers: LCCN 2017050223 | ISBN 9780815370789 (hardback : alk. paper)
Subjects: LCSH: Organizational change. | Corporate culture.
Classification: LCC HD58.8 .H36715 2018 | DDC 658.4/063--dc23
LC record available at https://lccn.loc.gov/2017050223

Visit the Taylor & Francis Web site at
http://www.taylorandfrancis.com

and the CRC Press Web site at
http://www.crcpress.com

I dedicate this book to my son Jim. He has grown up to be a man who radiates charm and respect. He is very caring, respectful, and not afraid to show his love and concern related to me. I am so proud of him. He has grown up to be the man I wanted to be.

Contents

SECTION III   Rewards and Recognition

SECTION V   Cultural Change Management (CCM)

SECTION VI   Summary

Recognition

I would like to recognize Ernst & Young, which first got me interested in Change Management. I also want to recognize Daryl Conner and his research and knowledge related to change management; in his field he has surpassed anyone I know of.

And, I would be remiss if I did not recognize Candy Rogers for taking my rough draft manuscript and transforming it into a completed manuscript by reforming it and correcting technical and grammatical errors.

Prologue

I don't know why you bought this book. You're already an expert in change management (CM). You are sitting there in your easy chair after years of experience in CM. You created something unique and different—something that no amount of innovation will ever be able to duplicate.

Certainly, our life is a miracle of change. The father's sperm cell attaches to an egg inside a small housing that has exactly the correct temperature controls to foster the change process. Almost immediately, the miracle of life begins forming as we start our change process. This process is going to create a unique output that no one has ever been able to duplicate, as we all have our little differences. Nine months later, the father will be giving out cigars to celebrate his child's coming into this marvelous world we live in. This transformation reaches its next phase when the doctor slaps the baby on the bottom and the baby begins to cry. The baby can cry because the change process allowed him or her to develop a means to make sounds. This miracle of birth is one of the most critical and complex CM processes a human is ever called upon to use. From that point on, each individual takes over his or her own change process until being transformed into a loving, caring adult.

For the first year of life, the change process takes place rapidly, as the baby still needs to be carried around. The next change allows a baby to stand holding onto something, and then soon a baby starts to crawl, walk, and then run. Progression may be made from a young child playing sports to a young adult coaching sports and then later in life an adult watching sports. These types of changes are natural and can be controlled. But during life, there are many times when it is very difficult to make certain changes, like to stop smoking and to drop those 25 extra pounds as your doctor suggests.

Unfortunately, at my stage in life, the same thing is true, only the order of the change activity is in reverse, like now I need to be carried around in a wheelchair. In between childhood and old age, we have the pleasure of enjoying all the good things in life that God has made available to us.

So you think you are an expert in managing how you change, and in these cases, an important part of your change is all controlled by you. But changes in the work environment often are an evaluation of the way someone else thinks you should behave. So start your romance with CM by managing some of the direct changes that impact you. Stop smoking. Lose 25 pounds and keep it off for 2 years. Become a vegetarian. You need to build up your personal resilience to change in the work environment. Most people are change bigots. They are all for change as long as it does not impact their behavioral patterns. The challenge is how effective you are at influencing other people to change their normal working and living behavior patterns.

In this book, I hope to provide you with a methodology that will be effective in helping you and other people embrace change at work and within the environment in which you exist. Change will make your trip through life more enjoyable and gratifying.

Think about how much more effectively you could manage the changes that impact you if you were the only human being on the earth. But alternatively, think about how lonesome it would be if no one cared if you're sick or well, win or lose, or succeed or fail. We are fortunate that we live in an environment that allows us to coexist with millions of other interesting individuals. There are those individuals you know, those you don't know, and those you are glad you don't know. But all of the change over the last 100 years has created an unsurpassed cultural environment than ever existed before. The only regret that I have is that I won't be here for another 100 years to enjoy the marvels that are yet to be discovered.

This book is designed to help organizations be more innovative, thereby making our advanced culture spread throughout the world. Someday in the future, people will be looking back at surgery going on in our hospitals thinking it was cruel and obsolete. Universities will be obsolete as we refine ways to directly pass knowledge from our computers into everyone's brain. Everybody in the world will be equally well educated, and the differences will be in how the education is used.

This book was particularly organized for organizations that want to stand out from the crowd and that hunger to obtain optimal results focusing on the 5P's:

- Pride. Employees are proud of their work and their organization.
- Performance. The entire organization operates at a high level of efficiency and effectiveness.
- Profit. The organization is profitable, thereby making it able to pay its employees a good salary, and pay higher than average dividends to its investors.

- Prestige. The organization is an admired place to work in and is known for its creative and high-quality products and services.
- Pleasure. Employees enjoy coming to work because they are doing something worthwhile in a friendly, supportive environment.

It has been said that only two things are inevitable—death and taxes. I would like to add the third thing—change. Even a guru sitting alone at the top of the mountain is undergoing change. That's why this individual climbed to the top of the mountain, so that he or she could see the world from a different view.

There are four types of changes:

1. Personal changes that impact you personally (e.g., aging, getting fired, divorce, illness, first child, and moral beliefs)
2. Social changes that impact the way you interface and react to other people on a social basis (e.g., getting married, child going to school, volunteer work with a not-for-profit organization, good friends, and interface and sales personnel at the grocery store)
3. Governmental-behavioral patterns that are dictated by a third party (e.g., Thou shall not steal, speed limits, paying taxes, behaviors, and church)
4. Occupational, including the way your organization reacts to changes in processes, products, and projects (e.g., release a new product, be assigned to a new manager, install a new software package, and adapt to a new organizational structure)

This book is designed to provide a methodology that will reduce waste as a result of implementing occupational changes (designing and implementing new products, processes, or organizational structure). This methodology is called *Innovative Change Management (ICM)*. ICM is further divided into two submethodologies (see Figure P.1):

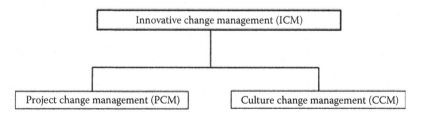

FIGURE P.1
Innovative change management.

- Project change management (PCM)
- Culture change management (CCM)

PCM is a methodology designed to work in conjunction with a project, program, organizational restructuring, and/or new product release. It is used in conjunction with a single item that has a start date and an end date, like a project or program (e.g., CCM is included in the project plan for the soon to be released M13 computer). Due to it being applied to a single entity and not across the organization, it was named PCM.

CCM is a methodology designed to penetrate into the organization's basic principles, visions, and operational habits. It usually makes use of a number of individual PCM projects that are implemented over a period of 1 or 2 years. We found that you can change the personality of an organization comparatively rapidly, but it can easily revert back to its old operating mode where the employees feel less stressed and more comfortable doing the same old thing in the same old way.

ICM is the integration of PCM and CCM in a way that they complement each other and minimize the risk of failures. If you implement too much change at one time, you can quickly send the organization into future shock, and it thus becomes nonfunctional. If you are carefully cautious and slowly introduce CM concepts into the organization, the change will be treated like normal business. ICM is designed to keep CM as the urgent activity without stressing the people affected by the change activities.

To get a real permanent change in the organization's culture, you need to use both PCM technology to minimize stress on project-by-project basis and CCM technology to bring about a lasting cultural change throughout the organization. Real cultural change occurs when you don't just change the way you do something, you do something because it has become a habit. It is not special; it's the way we do it here.

CCM requires some major changes in management styles (e.g., management needs to accept failure as a learning experience, and it needs to be willing to manage using a new set of redesigned vision, mission, and principles). CCM is designed to apply to everyone, even if they will not have the opportunity to serve as a member of a project or program team.

For many years, the major focus of the CM specialist was on ensuring the individual project is implemented with a minimum of disruption. This approach provides very positive results, as project success rates jumped by as much as 30%. Although an individual-based PCM methodology provided some excellent results that impressed the executive team, it had little or no effect on the organization's culture. Each time a new project came down, it had a new start because the impacted people often had never been involved in a PCM project or they had only been involved for a very short period of time many years before. PCM projects are designed to impact the targets' behaviors, but not their habits.

> Change behaviors to get something done. Change habits to sustain high levels of performance.

H. James Harrington

Author

 **Dr. H. James Harrington** is one of the world's quality system gurus with more than 60 years of experience. In the book, *Tech Trending*, Dr. Harrington was referred to as "the quintessential tech trender." *The New York Times* referred to him as having a "...knack for synthesis and an open mind about packaging his knowledge and experience in new ways—characteristics that may matter more as prerequisites for new-economy success than technical wizardry...." He has been involved in developing quality management systems in Europe, South America, North America, Middle East, Africa, and Asia.

Present Responsibilities:

Dr. H. James Harrington now serves as the chief executive officer for the Harrington Management Systems. He also serves as the chairman of the board for a number of businesses and as the U.S. Chairman of Chair on Technologies for Project Management at the University of Quebec in Montreal. Dr. Harrington is recognized as one of the world leaders in applying performance improvement methodologies to business processes.

Previous Experience:

In February 2002, Dr. Harrington retired as the COO of Systemcorp A.L.G., the leading supplier of knowledge management and project management software solutions. Prior to this, he served as a principal and one of the leaders in the Process Innovation Group at Ernst & Young. Dr. Harrington was with IBM for over 30 years as a senior engineer and project manager.

Dr. Harrington is past chairman and past president of the prestigious International Academy for Quality and of the American Society for

Quality Control. He is also an active member of the Global Knowledge Economics Council.

Credentials:

The Harrington/Ishikawa Medal presented yearly by the Asian-Pacific Quality Organization was named after Dr. Harrington to recognize his many contributions to the region. In 1997, the Quebec Society for Qualite named their Quality Award "The Harrington/Neron Medal" honoring Dr. Harrington for his many contributions to the Quality Movement in Canada. In 2000, the Sri Lanka national quality award was named after him. The Middle East and Europe Best Quality Thesis Award was named "The Harrington Best TQM Thesis Award". The University of Sudan has established a "Harrington Excellence Chair" to study methodologies to improve organizational performance. The Chinese government presented him with the Magnolia Award for his major contribution to improving the quality of Chinese products.

Dr. Harrington's contributions to performance improvement around the world have brought him many honors and awards, including the Edwards Medal, the Lancaster Medal, ASQ's Distinguished Service Medal, and many others. He was appointed the honorary advisor to the China Quality Control Association, and he was elected to the Singapore Productivity Hall of Fame in 1990. He has been named lifetime honorary President of the Asia Pacific Quality Organization and honorary Director of the Association Chilean de Control de Calidad.

Dr. Harrington has been elected a fellow of the British Quality Control Organization and the American Society for Quality Control. He was also elected an honorary member of the quality societies in Taiwan, Argentina, Brazil, Colombia, and Singapore. He is also listed in the "Worldwide Who's Who" and "Men of Distinction Worldwide." He has presented hundreds of papers on performance improvement and organizational management structure at the local, state, national, and international levels.

Dr. Harrington has two Doctor of Philosophy degrees—one in quality engineering and the other an honorary PhD in quality management.

Dr. Harrington is a very prolific author, publishing hundreds of technical reports and magazine articles. He has authored or coauthored over 55 books and 10 software packages. His e-mail address is hjh@ svinet.com.

BOOKS BY H. JAMES HARRINGTON

The following is a list of some of the many books that Harrington has authored and coauthored:

- The Improvement Process; 1987—one of 1987 best-selling business books
- Poor-Quality Cost; 1987
- Excellence—The IBM Way; 1988
- The Quality/Profit Connection; 1988
- Business Process Improvement; 1991—the first book on Process Redesign
- The Mouse Story; 1991
- Of Tails and Teams; 1994
- Total Improvement Management; 1995
- High Performance Benchmarking; 1996
- The Complete Benchmarking Workbook; 1996
- ISO 9000 and Beyond; 1996
- The Business Process Improvement Workbook; 1997
- The Creativity Toolkit—Provoking Creativity in Individuals and Organizations; 1998
- Statistical Analysis Simplified—The Easy-to-Understand Guide to SPC and Data Analysis; 1998
- Area Activity Analysis—Aligning Work Activities and Measurements to Enhance Business Performance; 1998
- ISO 9000 Quality Management System Design: Optimal Design Rules for Documentation, Implementation, and System Effectiveness (ISO 9000 Quality Management System Design) – coauthor; 1998
- Reliability Simplified—Going beyond Quality to Keep Customers for Life; 1999
- ISO 14000 Implementation—Upgrading Your EMS Effectively; 1999
- Performance Improvement Methods—Fighting the War on Waste; 1999
- Simulation Modeling Methods—An Interactive Guide to Results-Based Decision Making; 2000
- Project Change Management—Applying Change Management to Improvement Projects; 2000
- E-Business Project Manager; 2002

- Process Management Excellence—the Art of Excelling in Process Management; 2005
- Project Management Excellence—the Art of Excelling in Project Management; 2005
- Change Management Excellence—The Art of Excelling in Change Management; 2005
- Knowledge Management Excellence—The Art of Excelling in Knowledge Management; 2005
- Resource Management Excellence—The Art of Excelling in Resource Management; 2005
- Six Sigma Statistics Simplified; 2006
- Improving Healthcare Quality and Cost with Six Sigma; 2006
- Making Teams Hum; 2007
- Advanced Performance Improvement Approaches: Waging the War on Waste II; 2007
- Six Sigma Green Belt Workbook; 2008
- Six Sigma Yellow Belt Workbook; 2008
- Fast-Action Solution Technique published by Paton Professional; 2009
- Strategic Performance Improvement Approaches: Waging the War on Waste III; 2008
- Corporate Governance: From Small to Mid-Sized Organizations; 2009
- Streamlined Process Improvement; 2011
- The Organizational Alignment Handbook: A Catalyst for Performance Acceleration; 2011
- The Organizational Master Plan Handbook: A Catalyst for Performance Planning and Results; 2012
- Performance Accelerated Management (PAM): Rapid Improvement to Your Key Performance Drivers; 2013
- Closing the Communication Gap: An Effective Method for Achieving Desired Results; 2013
- Lean Six Sigma Black Belt Handbook: Tools and Methods for Process Acceleration; 2013
- Lean Management Systems Handbook; 2014
- Maximizing Value Propositions to Increase Project Success Rates; 2014
- Making the Case for Change: Using Effective Business Cases to Minimize Project and Innovation Failures; 2014

- Techniques and Sample Outputs That Drive Business Excellence; 2015
- Effective Portfolio Management Systems; 2015
- Change Management: Manage the Change or It Will Manage You; 2016
- Innovation Tools Handbook, Volume 1: Organizational and Operational Tools, Methods and Methodologies That Every Innovator Must Know; 2016
- The Innovation Tools Handbook, Volume 2: Evolutionary and Improvement Tools That Every Innovator Must Know; 2016
- The Innovation Tools Handbook, Volume 3: Creative Tools, Methods, and Techniques That Every Innovator Must Know; 2016
- Lean TRIZ: How to Dramatically Reduce Product-Development Costs with This Innovative Problem-Solving Tool; 2017

Section I

What Is Innovative Change Management (ICM)?

1

Introduction to Innovative Change Management

> You are part of the change parade. You can be the bandleader or you can be the one who sweeps up the horse droppings after the parade has passed. It's up to you.
>
> **H. J. Harrington**

We all like to think of ourselves as *change masters*, but, in truth, we are really *change bigots*. Everyone in the management supports change. They want to see others change, but when it comes to the managers themselves changing, they are reluctant to move away from their past experiences that have proven to be successful for them. If an organization is going to change, top management must be the first to do so.

In today's worldwide marketplace, customers don't have to settle for being second best. Overnight mail brings the best to everyone's doorstep. The Internet allows people to shop internationally, making it easy for them to get the best quality, reliability, and price the world can offer. Customers are concerned about the procurement cycle, but they are equally or more concerned about finding organizations that care, are quick to respond, and will listen and react to their unique needs. This means that to succeed in the twenty-first century, organizations must excel in all parts of their business. This means that every part of the organization is now faced with the challenge of making some extreme changes in the way they operate and what it will take to win over today's savvy customers.

Our environment is changing, our culture is changing, and the way we work is changing. The outside dynamics, technologies, strategies, and plans continuously change leaving us with only three options:

1. We can fight it and delay it, but we will change eventually.
2. We can ignore it and hope it will go away, but it will not, and we will be overcome by it.
3. We can embrace it, look forward to it, and thus find our assignment much more interesting, controllable, and enjoyable.

Our business world is in a never-ending cycle. We used to be able to work 8 hours a day, and when we shut down for the night, our competition also closed their doors. Not so today. When we close our doors at 6 pm, there is a competitor that is just starting his or her day. There is active competition for almost all products available online 24 hours a day.

- In the 1880s, most of our population was made up of *land workers*—individuals who planted corn, harvested wheat, raised cattle, and so on (see Figure 1.1).
- In the early 1900s, we left the farms to go to the city and work in factories. This brought on the formation of big business. The United States became a nation of *factory workers*.
- In the early 1920s, successful businesses grew to the point that they needed large office areas to support the work that was going on in factories. As a result, people's objectives were focused on becoming *office workers*.

FIGURE 1.1
Worker evolution.

- With the onset of World War II, factories required more knowledge-able people working in the support areas. This required the office worker to become a *knowledge worker*.
- With the invention of the Internet and computers now sitting on everyone's desk, we all had more knowledge at our disposal than ever before. As a result, the knowledge worker was quickly transformed into an *information worker*.
- In the twenty-first century, a group of specialists can be found in almost every field of business. Smokestack organizations optimized their parts of the business, causing these to become suboptimized. The computer along with the Internet minimized the amount of creativity that was required to be a satisfactory performer. Costly failures in new product development required a better understanding of the total process. Project management had gained in stature but still did not have the leverage to reduce the project failure rate to an acceptable level. Between 75% and 90% of all products that start on the project design cycle are successful. Often, individuals, who are creative by nature, do not understand the total new product development cycle and how to select the winning products and eliminate the losers early in the development cycle. As a result, the innovation age that we are presently living in came into being.

What is the next cycle going to be? That is anybody's guess. I'm betting it will be the home worker stage.

> It's not the strongest species that survive, nor the most intelligent, but the most responsive to change.
>
> **Charles Darwin**

OPENING THE DOOR TO CHANGE

Things change so rapidly that by the time I get my thoughts down on paper, they have changed. Almost everything is changing all the time. There are a few stubborn people who honestly believe that the way they were doing something last year is still the best way to do it today. These individuals usually are people who work for mediocre companies who follow the industry trends, rather than leading the trends. I have one friend who still watches black-and-white TV because he believes that color TV is just a fad. A girl I know wears bobbed hair because long hair is too hard to care for, and yet she is very concerned that young men are not asking her out on a date. She's just good old Mary. I still have my high school letter sweater hoping that someday I'll get a chance to wear it. I prefer to take my family on vacation to Disneyland, not Disney World. Why?—Because I know what to do, where to go, and how to get to the Haunted House at Disneyland. We all want to hold onto the things we are doing, because we don't feel comfortable taking a chance on something new and different.

The world is full of challenges and opportunities, which allows us to make vast sums of money and to meet new and interesting people. However, instead, too many of us come home from work to read the paper, watch TV, and just have a pizza with the family. Many of us feel that this is all it takes to make our world, and if that is your case, you live in a very small world. It's a world where you're walking in the field of hundred dollar bills and are too lazy to bend down and pick them up. If that is your world, the only mark you will leave on the world is a tombstone.

There's a nice comfortable feeling about doing something that you know you can do, but there is a huge amount of excitement, fun, and adventure in challenging the unknown and trying something different or recognizing a need and fulfilling it. You may not become a multimillionaire or you may go bankrupt if the adventure you undertake does not pan out. Either way, take it from a man who is almost 90 years old. If you don't try to change and go out of your way to change, you will be left with just memories of what you should have and could have done. Take a chance—I did and I can assure you that the feelings of accomplishment will more than make up for the effort and risk.

CHANGE IS ALWAYS PERSONAL

Change is a very personal thing. Each individual is changing and is affected by change every day. Our view of other people, organizations, and countries is based on the situation to which we have been subjected. As the environment around us changes, we change also. At times the environmental changes can cause our thinking to do a 180° turn around. This change may not always be in a positive direction. Figure 1.2 depicts

FIGURE 1.2
Change is not always positive.

the difference between how a woman and a man perceive each other as they go from courtship to marriage and to divorce.

Less than 50% of the workforce is now employed in full-time jobs. Many are working in temporary or part-time jobs, either because they want it that way or because that is all that is available. The really new trend is for people to be self-employed or to do consulting work. Many individuals who are out of work now call themselves "consultants." It's almost as though today's definition of a consultant is "a person who doesn't have a job but is looking for one."

The future belongs to those who believe in the beauty of their dreams.

Eleanor Roosevelt
Past First Lady of the United States

IMPORTANT DEFINITIONS USED IN THIS BOOK

Just to be sure that we have a common understanding related to the key terms used in innovative change management (ICM), we begin this chapter with the following important definitions:

Definitions

- **Change** is a perceived departure from what was expected. Change is disruptive when a large gap exists between what happened and what was experienced.

- **Culture** are the beliefs, behaviors, and assumptions shared by individuals within the organization, which include such things as procedures, values, and unspoken norms.
- **Culture change management (CCM)** focuses on the human side of change as it affects employees in their day-to-day work activities by creating a resilient culture. CCM emphasizes that it is the people who make the change happen (or not, in some cases), and their ability to adapt, absorb, and assimilate new ways of operating, which ultimately defines success. It is a methodology that is designed to minimize the negative impact of social, organizational, process, or product changes on the total organization or a specific function within the organization. It focuses on the culture of the organization rather than on the individual project.
- **ICM** is a disciplined framework for driving business results by changing behaviors. It entails managing the effect of new business processes, changes in organizational structure, or cultural changes within an enterprise. The challenge is to apply effective practices to anticipate and minimize resistance to change. It is the combination of project change management (PCM) and CCM.
- **Organization** is a company, corporation, firm, enterprise, or association or any part thereof, whether incorporated or not, public or private, that has its own function and administration (source ISO 8402:1994).
- **PCM** is the application of change management (CM) methodologies to an individual project to increase its probability of being successful. It is a methodology used to minimize the social, organizational, process, or product changes that could impact the successful implementation of a specific project or program. It does not include job changes to the specific project or program.
- **Project management** is the application of knowledge, skills, tools, and techniques to project activities to meet project requirements. Project management is accomplished through the
  - Application and integration of project management
  - Processes of initiating, planning, executing, monitoring, controlling, and closing
- **Stakeholder** is an individual or group of individuals or organizations with a common interest. Stakeholders of an organization typically are the customers, owners, employees, employees' families, suppliers, and consumers.

This book is a solid resource for people who need to make change happen. It is a tactical, hands-on guide that will lead you through the steps of the entire process from planning for a change through sustaining the new ways in your organization.

TWO TYPES OF ICM

Although many consultants and authorities have different views about how an ICM system should be put in place and operate, all of these views fall into two general categories of ICM:

- PCM
- CCM

PCM Advantages

Most experts have developed processes that support the PCM approach. There are many advantages to using this approach, as it develops customized PCM approaches that are often unique to the individual project. Additionally, the PCM approach allows the methodology to be customized to the needs and objectives of the specific project. It typically relates to breaking down resistance to the change in the impacted area. This allows the PCM methodology to address the activities and people who are directly impacted by the project. The real purpose of PCM is to minimize the time required to recover from change and to reduce the stress on the employees during the change period. Figure 1.3 portrays the stress levels and impact times for two different projects—Project A (a more complex project than Project B so as a result, its stress levels are higher) and Project B.

You will notice in Figure 1.3 that the stress on the employee increases extremely rapidly once the employee finds out that the change is going to impact him or her. It remains there while the employee is collecting information related to the potential change. Once the employee understands how the change will impact him or her and the change has been implemented, the employee's stress level gradually decreases until the employee gains confidence in his or her ability to do the assignment.

Section IV of this book focuses on how to manage projects successfully using PCM. Using the PCM methodology is the correct starting point

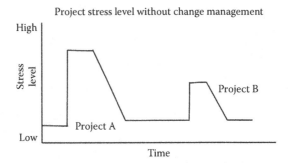

FIGURE 1.3
Typical project stress curve.

for all organizations except those that have a great deal of experience using ICM. I personally believe that PCM is less important than CCM. CCM looks at change from a broader standpoint focusing on changing the culture within an organization, not just preparing the people who will be affected by a change for a specific program or project. Because PCM focuses on individual projects, it gets results much faster than CCM and serves as an effective short-term example of how ICM will improve the organization's performance. The disadvantage of PCM is that it only impacts a small portion of the organization's population. PCM provides an excellent foundation for the shift in the organization's culture using CCM.

CCM Advantages

The CCM approach addresses the total change needs of the organization. It builds a common understanding and approach to the ever-changing environment we are in today. It is usually implemented in parallel with PCM but addresses the total population of employees, rather than just the employees who are impacted by a specific change. It is directed at building the foundation that allows individual changes to be absorbed into the organization with a very minimal amount of destruction. The large curve for "Project A" in Figure 1.4 shows the stress level for a typical project without having applied the PCM methodology. The small curve for "Project A" in Figure 1.4 shows the stress level for the same project with PCM methodology applied to it. Note that the first curve stress level in Figure 1.4 drives the targeted people into dysfunctional behavior without

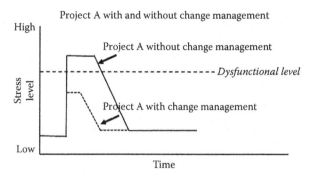

FIGURE 1.4
Impact of CCM.

ICM. The second curve's maximum stress level is well below the dysfunctional performance level for the affected area because ICM was applied. It is important to point out that if these were different projects going on in the same location, the total stress would be the sum of the two stress levels. It's important to point out that organizations may be going through a number of cultural changes at the same time.

The transformation from an information worker to an innovation worker requires a major change in the organization's behavior patterns and culture. This requires that a homogeneous plan for a culture change be prepared to make the organization competitive. Almost every performance improvement methodology (TQM, ISO 9000, process redesign, lean, supply chain, Six Sigma, customer focus, etc.) that has been developed over the last 50 years pleaded with the reader to change the organization's culture in order for the improvement method to function effectively. It's very important that the individual desired shifts in culture are blended together to provide the single combined culture required to make the organization competitive.

IMPLEMENTING PCM

Over time everything changes—even our underwear style has gone through a cycle (see Figure 1.5). We recommend that an organization starts its ICM activities using the PCM methodology. This allows the organization to develop skills and confidence in their ability to manage

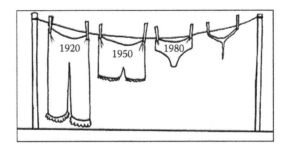

FIGURE 1.5
Things change with time.

resistance to change and to prepare employees for living in a new, changed environment. An additional advantage is that PCM activities usually only last a month or so. The CCM takes months to implement, and its activities are measured by the willingness of your employees to embrace change as part of the normal work environment. Many companies are bringing together their suggestion department, CM, human resources department, and innovation management activities to form a new department called "Opportunity Center" that serves as the foundation for the change and improvement activities within the organization. At first this may seem like a strange combination of responsibilities, but when you think about it, all of these functions are focused on developing the employees' capabilities. The Opportunity Center focuses on developing increased creativity and innovation throughout the organization. It will help any employee document his or her concept and help sell the concepts that meet the organization's requirements to become a project. It also aids the employee in presenting it to the proper level of management. Often the Opportunity Center helps teams develop their value proposition.

MAGNITUDE OF CHANGE ACTIVITIES

The magnitude of the change initiative can be divided into three categories (see Figure 1.6):

- *First-order magnitude* change only affects the tasks that are being performed as they relate to the technology, but have little or no impact on the culture, structure, and people. It is a translation

The magnitude of driven change

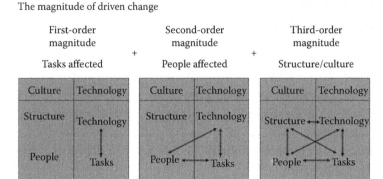

FIGURE 1.6
Magnitude of the different types of change initiatives.

of the technology change into the tasks to keep up with the latest methodologies.

- *Second-order magnitude* change affects the people who are involved with the change. It is a combination of culture and technology. The three elements involved are people, tasks, and technology. You can see that the complexity has increased by 300%.

- *Third-order magnitude* change is the most complex. It increases the highest stress level and meets with the most resistance. It involves all the culture and technology (people, structure, etc.) issues. As you can see from Figure 1.6, the complexity of implementing a third-order change has increased by over 600%. When we talk about bringing about a change in the organization's culture or establishing shared visions throughout the organization, we are addressing third-order magnitude change. Third-order magnitude change almost always requires the support of a very effectively implemented PCM approach to make it successful.

When your project's objective is to develop a shared vision or any other projects that involve structure, technology, people, and tasks the culture they are dealing with, it is a third-order change. This means that PCM is one of the most important methodologies that your project management team has to master. Often major projects have a change agent assigned very early in the cycle.

Research confirms that as much as 60% of change initiatives and other projects fail as a direct result of a fundamental inability to manage their social implications.

PCM CYCLE

The following are the six phases that make up a PCM project:

- Phase 1. Cultural or project assessment
- Phase 2. Inclusion of CM in the organization's vision, values, and objectives
- Phase 3. Development of a PCM plan and combination of that with the project plan
- Phase 4. Pre-implementation activities
- Phase 5. Implementation activities
- Phase 6. Measurement of results

The Status Quo Level

The status quo (AS/IS condition or present state) is an established pattern of expectations. It is characterized by a relatively stable and familiar environment. It represents a dynamic equilibrium that continues indefinitely until a force disrupts it. As the rate of change increases, the present state transforms from a static into a fluid state. We spend most of our life in the status quo or present-state environment. But change may cause expectations to be disrupted. They can be positive or negative changes or disruptions. People feel comfortable and secure living in the status quo environment. They may not like everything they are doing (nobody does), but at least they know what to do and they know they can do it. This provides the individual with security and a sense of purpose. Everyone wants to hold onto the status quo state because during change the 4Cs take over a big portion of their lives. These 4Cs are as follows:

- Confidence
- Competence
- Control
- Comfort

These 4Cs create a very unstable mental environment for most of your people. Even though the change is still in the planning stage, productivity falls off for the targeted managers and employees as they spend more and more of their time discussing how this unknown thing will affect them

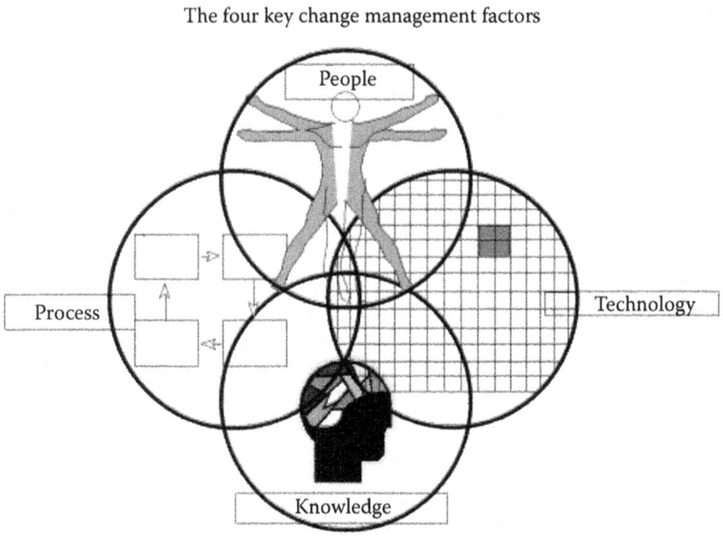

The four key change management factors

FIGURE 1.7
Key CM forces.

and brooding over its impact. Disruption of any one of the 4Cs causes the following disruptions within the organization:

- Low stability
- High stress
- Declining productivity
- Anxiety
- Fatigue
- Increased conflict

The Four Key ICM Factors

In today's fast-changing environment, the ICM methodologies are directed at juggling four balls at the same time. They are people, processes, knowledge, and technology (see Figure 1.7). Each of these four balls reacts differently when being juggled. Because they don't follow the normal path, it makes the juggling act far more difficult.

The transformation to an innovative organization rests right in the middle of where these four key ICM forces overlap each other. Adding the need for a major cultural change from the information workforce to an innovative workforce is the fifth key ICM factor that needs to be considered and dealt with.

Keeping the correct balance between these four balls is becoming more difficult as the work environment becomes more complex. Typical things that make the four ICM forces more difficult to handle and control are as follows:

- More interactive components (e.g., people, tasks, issues, problems, and opportunities)
- More interdependence among the components
- More unanticipated consequences
- Less time to react to events
- Less predictability and control
- Less durability of solutions
- A higher level of education for the average employee

With all of these changes coming at us from different directions, we have to be careful that we do not saturate our employees' capabilities to handle their assignments. We also must be careful to be sure that the employees' stress level is not reaching the saturation point where they become dysfunctional.

Definition

Dysfunctional: Any change-related activity or feeling that diverts resources away from meeting productivity and quality standards.

KEY GUIDELINES

One key phrase that guides my ICM work with clients is: "Today's view of the future is largely based upon past experience." When a higher percentage of the projects started down through the innovative cycle fail to meet their profit objectives, it provides us with an excellent opportunity to improve project management. This improvement needs to start long before the project starts with the implementation cycle. Some of the factors that cause projects to fail often before they reach the consumer are as follows:

- Changes to the project scope
- Unsolved problem or unexploited opportunity
- Overoptimistic value propositions

- Lack of project management and ICM skills
- Wasted time, money, and people resources
- No or minimal return on investment (no value added)
- Lower morale
- Rush to start the project without sufficient research to understand impact on the customer and the organization
- Poor market research
- Threatened job security for those involved
- Organization's loss of confidence in its leadership when management does not successfully fulfill the promise of their announced intention
- Ignored management directives

2

The AS/IS Environment

PROJECT CHANGE MANAGEMENT ADDRESSES PEOPLE PROBLEMS

In Figure 2.1 Daryl Conner gives some good advice. I have worked on hundreds of different consulting engagements implementing total quality management (TQM), business process improvement, organization alignment, project management, organization restructuring, and Six Sigma, with some marvelous success in each of these methodologies. I also had miserable failures. Basically these were always implemented in about the same fashion. They all had training and management support initially; all they needed was to have a project to apply the methodology to. After carefully analyzing wins and losses, it became obvious to me that all of these methodologies are good and will work. When they don't work, it is not the methodology that failed, it's the way it was implemented. We don't say that TQM failed, business process improvement failed, or Six Sigma failed. It wasn't the methodology that failed; it was the people or the organization that did not use the methodology correctly. We don't say that management failed, or the employee failed, or the consultants failed. We say the failure was the methodology, because we don't want to put the blame for the failure on the real cause of failure—the way we implement the methodology. Each of these methodologies works if they have the proper executive support, management sponsorship, and employee acceptance and involvement. Each incident needs to be customized to the unique situation within the organization. If you buy a car and expect it to travel 480 mph, the car is going to be considered a failure. In fact, the car is an excellent way of traveling if you're going to obey the speed limits. If you need to go 480 mph, you bought the wrong methodology; you should've bought a jet airplane.

"It is inadequate to manage just project cost, schedule, and quality. Without managing the project's social impact, most projects will fail to reach their full potential."

Daryl R. Conner

FIGURE 2.1
Daryl R. Conner, consultant and author.

Every manager needs to be a salesperson for all improvement initiatives that the organization decides to invest in. It's often the way the change is presented rather than the change itself that is the problem. For example, a man comes in to look at buying a new car. He likes the car; it is the right color, right size, and not too expensive. He notices a gadget on the steering wheel and asks the salesperson, "What is this? What does it do?" The salesperson replies, "Oh, that's the cruise control; it will keep you from driving too fast." After some time kicking the tires, the potential customer decides to look at another brand before he makes his choice. So he looks at another car, which is about equivalent to the first car (i.e., right features, right color, good gas mileage, comfortable seats, and not too expensive). This time he asks the salesperson, "What does the gadget on the steering wheel do?" This salesman replies, "That's something you will really like. It's called a 'cruise control.' You are a salesman and you will be on the road a high percentage of your working hours. You can set it for the speed you want to travel at, and it will automatically adjust the car speed to the desired level. It's a huge advantage in keeping you from slowly increasing your speed to the point that the state police pulls you over. With this you just decide how fast you want to go and set it for that speed, and you can relax and take your foot off the gas pedal and the car will continue at a constant speed until you put your foot on the brake." Understandably, the man bought the second car.

Two of the major reasons for project failure are not preparing management to adequately support the project and also not convincing the employees they should look forward to using the new methods. Just think of when you buy a new car, how good you feel about driving it. Why? Because you're getting something newer, cleaner, and with fewer problems than the car you are driving today. The changes that were implemented within the organization need to entice our employees' and managers' emotions the same as that new car does. As we talk about innovative change management (ICM), we should focus on the human aspects of implementing and using something different.

INNOVATION AREAS

In analyzing innovation activities, we find that there are five major innovation areas that are used in most projects:

1. Management
2. Products
3. Processes
4. Marketing and sales
5. Support services

To change the organization's culture, there needs to be change in behavior and habits in these five major innovation areas. To accomplish this, we suggest using the McKinsey 7Ss model with an additional three drivers that we feel need to be added. (The McKinsey 7Ss model was developed in the 1980s by McKinsey consultants Tom Peters, Robert Waterman, and Julien Philips, with help from Richard Pascale and Anthony G. Athos.) We refer to the following as the "10Ss" model. The first 7Ss are based on the McKinsey 7Ss methodology. It's easy to see how these 7Ss (7 key innovation drivers) can have a major impact on employee and management behavior and habits. As we prepared detailed plans to improve for each of the 7Ss, we realized that there were three more key innovation drivers (systematic change management, specialized technology/information technology systems, and situated knowledge management) that were necessary in order for McKinsey's 7Ss improvement approach to work effectively.

Definition

10Ss model—This is a combination of the McKinsey 7Ss model plus three additional key innovation drivers added by the author. Each cultural driver must be considered when an organization or part of the organization is considering a major change or a high-risk change. Even with low risk, minor changes such as these 10 key innovation drivers should be considered in developing the implementation plan, although specific emphasis may not be required in many cases.

The 10Ss model included the following:

1. *Shared vision*—Review and update, if necessary, the organization's purpose and principles.
2. *Strategy*—Define the approach that will be used to bring about the desired cultural change.
3. *Systems*—These are the efficiency and effectiveness of the critical business processes.
4. *Structure*—Organize the way the impacted areas are restructured to support the proposed cultural change.
5. *Skills*—An individual's education and life experiences help to develop his or her skills that are critical for his or her quality of work life and existence. How do you select the right skills for the particular job assignments in the impacted areas?
6. *Style/personality*—This is the impression that a person leaves after he or she comes in contact with someone. Most people have many different personalities based on their environment and the individuals involved. It is the style that makes up an individual work area based on how each individual interfaces with each other. The manager's style usually has the biggest impact on the impacted area.
7. *Staffing*—What are the criteria for the affected area?
8. *Systematic change management*—This determines how to minimize resistance to the cultural change and prepare the organization for future changes.
9. *Specialized technology/information technology systems*—This is the effective use of information technology to handle the boring repetitive jobs and increase value added per employee.
10. *Situated knowledge management (knowledge management)*—This is the way knowledge is generated, captured, documented, and communicated throughout the organization. Knowledge is a mixture

of experience, practices, traditions, values, contextual information, expert insight, and interpretation that provides an environment and framework for evaluating and incorporating new experiences and information. It is divided into two major categories: explicit and tacit. Knowledge management is a strategy that turns an organization's intellectual assets, both recorded information and the talents of its members, into greater productivity, new values, and increased competitiveness.

TODAY'S EMPLOYEE

Ann Landers wrote in one of her columns, "Anyone who believes that the competitive spirit in America is dead has never been in a supermarket when a cashier opens another checkout line." Yes, people are competitive in nature, but too often we put away that competitive spirit when we enter the organization's front door. We become part of the pack. We are afraid to stand out as individuals. We don't want to be enthusiastic about our job because the other employees will think we are strange, but enthusiasm makes the ordinary person extraordinary. As individuals, we all have the same needs that must be fulfilled if we are going to excel at our job. They are as follows:

- *Economic security.* We need to feel that we are getting a fair day's pay for a fair day's work.
- *Personal self-esteem.* We all want to be viewed as value added to the organization. None of us wants to be average.
- *Personal self-worth.* We need to feel that we are contributing to a worthwhile goal.
- *Personal contribution.* We want to be listened to—to have our ideas heard. We can accept the fact that everything we suggest may not be implemented, but we need a fair hearing.
- *Personal recognition.* We all need feedback to show that good work is appreciated, that what we are doing is worthwhile.
- *Emotional security.* We all need to be able to trust the managers we work for and to feel that they will be honest with us.

Only when these six basic needs are satisfied can an individual have a chance at excelling at his or her assigned task(s).

That's Not Fair

The employee does not expect the world to be fair because it isn't. Those who dwell on the unfairness in life use it as an excuse for their lack of drive and success. No matter where you are in the world, there will always be people above you who are not as deserving as you are (in your eyes), and people at your level or below who do not do their fair share. Most of us believe that we have more than our fair share of problems. In truth, there are many people who have overcome more obstacles than we will ever face and have become more successful than we will ever be. They have used these obstacles to build stamina and the drive to succeed, to forge a will and personality that are unstoppable.

But, there are many individuals who have had much lighter burdens to carry than we have faced, who have failed miserably. No, the world is not fair, but employees accept and understand this fact. We all need to make the best use of our talents and opportunities to provide ourselves with a positive attitude and a personal dedication and commitment to success. It will make life much easier and more joyful. Look at your cup as half full, not half empty.

The Open-Minded Employee

In today's environment, growth is going to be very limited. Management and employees need to look for other ways to stimulate job satisfaction and recognition. Employees need to have a very open mind about what is going on around them and how they can contribute. Employees who do not find their job interesting are employees who have closed minds to its possibilities.

Employees and managers alike make excuses for their closed minds. Some of the more frequently used excuses are as follows: "We tried that before." "Let's hold it at bay." "Let's give it more thought." "Management would never do it." "You can't teach an old dog new tricks." It is time to open your minds and stop using these phrases. Every time you utter or hear one of these popular phrases, it's time to challenge what's going on. Stop putting up roadblocks and detour signs to change and start knocking them down. Ask yourself, "How can I make it work now if it didn't work before?" Ask if it isn't time you tried something new if it is a first-time suggestion. Embrace the positive, and cut the legs out from under the negative. You may not always win, but you will never win if you never try.

He worked by day
And toiled by night.
He gave up play
And some delight.
Dry books he read,
New things to learn.
And forged ahead
Success to earn.
He plodded on
With faith and pluck
And when he won
Others called it luck.

Unknown Author

3

Important Background

BUILDING COMMITMENT

Building commitment within all of the projects' stakeholders is essential, but few project managers seem to understand how important it is and know how to do it. They also don't know how easily it can be eroded. The commitment process is made up of three phases:

- Phase 1—Preparation
- Phase 2—Acceptance
- Phase 3—Commitment

Each of these three phases represents a critical juncture in the commitment process. Each phase has a number of degrees of support (stages) for the change project (see Table 3.1).

As an individual or organization moves from one stage to the next, the commitment to the change increases. Also, the degree of effort and time required to invest in the innovative change management (ICM) process increases based on the degree of commitment required to support the change project. Figure 3.1 depicts the pluses and minuses for each stage in the commitment model.

When implementing major change, there is a continuum of ICM strategies that can be used depending on the change and the degree of acceptance that the change must have for the targets. At one end of the commitment level is "internalized commitment," and at the other end is "institutionalized commitment," which is forced compliance (see Figure 3.2). It requires approximately 100% more change management effort to move from Stage 7: Institutionalization to Stage 8: Internalization.

TABLE 3.1

Commitment Model

Phase I: Preparation
- Stage 1: Contact
- Stage 2: Awareness

Phase II: Acceptance
- Stage 3: Understanding
- Stage 4: Positive Perception

Phase III: Commitment
- Stage 5: Installation
- Stage 6: Adoption
- Stage 7: Institutionalization
- Stage 8: Internalization

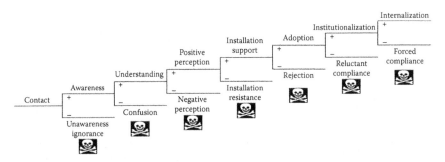

FIGURE 3.1
Stages in the commitment model: pluses and minuses.

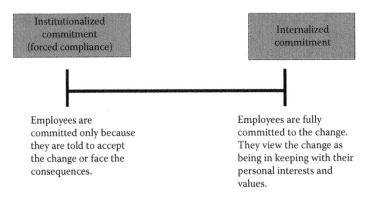

FIGURE 3.2
Comparison between Stage 7: Institutionalization and Stage 8: Internalization.

Institutionalized Commitment

Not all changes require the people who are affected by the change to believe in the change. They may only be required to comply with the change. These changes that are forced on the targets may be accepted by the targets because they wish to comply with the organization's activities. The organization motivates the targets to comply by rewarding those who comply and punishing the individuals who do not comply. Targets often mimic acceptable behaviors and learn to do and say what they consider acceptable to the organization. Of course, this approach does not have a positive impact on the target's attitude toward the change. In today's fast-changing environment, most organizations are realizing that their employees need to understand and support the change. With institutionalized commitment, the return on investment is often greatly reduced.

Internalized Commitment

Definition

Target—sometimes called "impacted employee"
The target is the individual or group affected by the change.

Internalized commitment occurs when the targets believe that the change reflects their personal beliefs, needs, and wants, as well as those of the organization. This level of commitment results in the targets taking ownership for the success of the change because it satisfied their own needs and they believe it is good for the organization. At the personal level, the change is more embraced and supported than the organization could ever mandate.

COMMUNICATION

To change the culture, we need to convince everyone that change is happening throughout the organization, near to them, and to them, on a day-to-day basis. Management should focus on developing an attitude within the organization that things are not quite right if things are not changing. Employees should question if they have been doing an assignment for the last 2 years the same way, isn't there something they can do or recommend to improve the process? A very effective communication system is the best way to accomplish this. This is one way of making everyone in the organization aware of what is going on around them. Make the most out of every idea that is implemented by sharing it with the rest of the organization so that they can see how things are changing in other parts of the organization. Put out a quarterly newsletter highlighting things that are happening within the organization. There is no such thing as a product release that is too small. Each new product release should be treated as a special occasion, giving a chance for the employees to come together and share in the excitement. We need to focus on the excitement of change, rather than on the problems related to change. Focus your communication on what individuals have done to improve the processes and their performance. Use regular town meetings to talk about the changes that are occurring and the challenges that we will have if we do not change. Use poster campaigns to give credit to individuals active in the change process. You will be surprised at how hard individuals try to create new ideas if there is a chance that his or her picture will be on a poster.

Five-Way Communications

Organizations have been trying desperately to establish effective two-way communications (up and down), and just as they have started to make real progress, they find that this was not adequate. Many organizations are now trying to establish five-way communications (up, down, horizontal, customer, and supplier). This five-way or star communication process is a key part of a participative team environment that is based on a strong supplier–customer relationship (see Figure 3.3).

Each line in Figure 3.3 represents a two-way communication route. For example, the line that runs between numbers 1 and 2 forms a two-way communication indicating that 1 communicates with 2 and 2 communicates with 1.

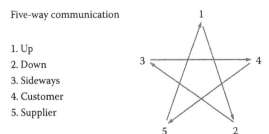

FIGURE 3.3
Five-way communications.

Today, the complex organizational environment makes this five-way communication system an essential part of an effective operation. In our information-rich society, management can no longer ration out just the information they believe that the employee needs to know. Likewise, every employee has an obligation to maintain active communication with all of his or her interfaces. The day of management being responsible for keeping the employee informed disappeared when we began to empower employees. Management's responsibility is to provide the communication process and media. It is everyone's responsibility to use it. Everyone has a personal responsibility to manage the communication network within their own star. At a minimum, every employee is involved in four of five points of the star. The actions that need to be taken to effectively make the five-way communication process work are as follows:

- Management needs to trust employees with information previously restricted to management.
- Management must establish the process.
- Everyone needs to be trained on how to use it.
- A reward system needs to be put in place to encourage the use of the process.

Today, technology and personal initiatives can easily take care of the communication problem if they are both used correctly. Computer networks, voice mail, centralized databases, telecommunication, videoconferencing, town hall meetings, and bowling leagues are just some of the means of communication; the list goes on and on. The five-way communication process in today's environment is not only desirable; it is mandatory.

One of the weaknesses in most communication systems is the inability or reluctance of the employees to use it. In most organizations, communication training has been limited to managers. This was a very realistic approach in a one-way, downward communication process. Why would you want to train employees in communication skills? If they knew how to communicate, they would want to be listened to, and who had time to do that? But today, with everyone having shared responsibilities in making the communication process work, everyone needs to be trained in how to use it and have access to the required media. The biggest problem we face in establishing a five-way communication process is getting the data into the process. A well-designed data system that is user friendly will group information into relative packages that minimize the time and effort required to obtain needed information.

The biggest roadblock to making this happen is upper management who, for years, have believed that information is power and were unwilling to share this power with their employees. Add to this the feeling that most employees cannot be trusted or are not intelligent enough to understand the business, and it is easy for management to justify not putting most of the information they control into the communication process. The fact of the matter is that most employees can be trusted, and the ones who cannot be trusted have already found ways to get the information they want.

There are many effective ways of getting a shared vision going within an organization, for example,

- You can print the vision statement on the back of everyone's business card.
- You can get everyone name holders for their desk with their name and the vision statement printed on it.
- You can give out printed copies of the vision statement.
- You can print the vision statement on every paycheck.
- You can prepare a screensaver that automatically comes up on any computer that is being used. Use this same screensaver to transmit activities and accomplishments related to the vision statement.
- Put up billboards with the employee's picture on it and the vision statement.

THE DOWNSIDE TO IMPROVEMENT (LAYOFFS)

It all sounds too good to be true. All you have to do is use the appropriate improvement approaches and ICM tools in the correct sequence, and quality and productivity will soar. Everyone will earn more money, and it is a win-win situation for all stakeholders. Theoretically, that is true under ideal conditions, but unfortunately in many organizations, that is not the reality of life. It probably is true if you can grow your market and market share at a rate that is equal to or faster than your productivity increase. However, if the market is constant and productivity improves, someone, somewhere, has to be put out of a job. Maybe that someone is not in our organization if you are growing your market share in a stagnant market at a rate that offsets the productivity improvement within the organization, but in some other competitive organization, there could be a negative impact.

In the ideal situation, increased productivity allows prices to be reduced, resulting in a larger market for everyone to feed upon. The reality of today is that most organizations improve to stay in business. As a result, improvements in productivity and quality often allow the organization to operate with fewer and fewer people because the market has not expanded fast enough to consume the additional output. The reality of not being able to maintain full employment has been realized by even the best organizations around the world. Some of the very best around the world face the problem of laying off surplus employees. Companies like Google, Apple, Toyota, and Boeing all, at one time or another, have needed to lay off surplus employees.

At this very early stage of implementing an improvement methodology, management needs to step up to the reality that as performance improves, jobs probably will be eliminated, and they have to decide what will be done with these surplus employees. If management has been running a tight ship, they probably can adopt a "no-layoff policy." Typically, these policies read something like this:

> *No-Layoff Policy:* No one will be laid off because of a quality or productivity improvement. People whose jobs are eliminated will be retrained for equivalent or more responsible jobs. This does not mean that it may not be necessary to lay employees off due to a business downturn.

When President Clinton was governor of Arkansas, he pushed the 1991 Legislative Session to pass quality management legislation. The law included the following provisions:

- Assured that no state employee will lose employment because of quality management efficiencies
- Provided ways to reallocate funds to support the quality movement within agencies
- Created a Quality Management Board

So what happens if you cannot afford to issue a no-layoff policy and your market does not grow sufficiently to keep your employees fully utilized? Is your only option a layoff? No, there are at least 20 other options that should be considered first. Some of them are as follows:

1. Increased customer demands
2. Deadwood removal

3. Overtime reduction
4. Skills training
5. Attrition
6. Train-the-trainer
7. Increased marketing and sales efforts
8. Voluntary leaves
9. Job rotation
10. Incentive retirement programs
11. Shorter work week
12. External schools
13. Civic programs
14. Employee relocation
15. Job sharing
16. Contract workers

THE FUTURE OF ICM

Executives around the world are now looking at building a culture that supports creativity and innovation. The organization's culture is the base that drives loyalty, the decisions we make, how we do our job, our creativity, our leadership, our communications, and our collaborations. It is one of the major impacts that has direct influence on how we are affected by the change. Over the years, the individuals who have been driving the change methodologies have tried to convince the Project Management Institute (PMI) that project change management (PCM) should be a separate item in the project methodology. Unfortunately, we have not been successful in making that happen.

ICM has distanced itself from PCM so that it can be applied to all types of changes in personnel, sales and marketing, and legal. This puts the ICM methodology in a position where its scope is much larger than the scope of the project management team. ICM, unlike PCM, is a long iterative process that frequently takes 3–5 years to implement and get the desired results. As a result, organizations should continue to use PCM while they are implementing ICM. PCM methodology and the project management methodology support each other like a glass supports water. Each of them can be disappointing by themselves, but together they are very satisfying.

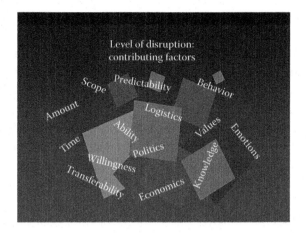

FIGURE 3.4
The contributing factors to disruption.

The depth and breadth of the ICM methodology penetrates into every part of the organization. Involved in making the transformation would be research, development, manufacturing, personnel, finance, after-sales services, sales, and marketing. Having a common cultural change methodology would be beneficial, but in most organizations, each function is faced with a different set of problems and personalities, which makes it necessary to customize the ICM methodology to the function's specific needs. It impacts factors such as those listed in Figure 3.4. You probably would not want the same level of innovation and risk applied to finance that you would apply to standard operating procedures in research and development.

Our studies indicate that there is a direct correlation between the employee's levels of satisfaction and enthusiasm related to the company and his or her ability to accept high stress levels of change without causing disruption to the organization. This quickly leads to an understanding that the impact change has on the organization is based on two factors:

1. Management's influence over the morale and loyalty of the individuals who work for them.
2. Their past experience with change and its impact and success rate.

In other words, it is as simple as, "Does management consider the employees an expense or an asset?"

H. J. Harrington

This requires the organization to collect four types of information:

1. What are the prejudices that are built into the individual employee's frame of reference? Are they based on projects they have been involved with before? This analysis is usually done by a history of change management survey.

2. What are the innovation strengths and weaknesses in your major innovation centers (management, product, process, and after-sales service, support areas, sales and marketing)? This question is usually answered by performing an Innovation Maturity Assessment related to each of the major innovation centers.

3. What does the employee like about the organization, and where does the employee feel there is an opportunity for improvement? This information is normally collected as part of an Employee Opinion Survey.

4. How do you define and measure the behavioral patterns for individuals who are complying with the innovation values and vision statement? A list of desired behavioral patterns should be developed well before the project is being implemented. It is very difficult and time consuming to measure behavioral patterns for an individual's compliance to the desired behaviors. As a result, it often primarily is measured by management's impression of how the desired behavior is changing the way management and employees react to each other. This is usually done by personal observations made by executive management. In some organizations, we worked with the executive team to install a self-measurement and reporting system. If an individual's action is not in line with the desired habit, the individual records it as a deviation in performance. It is not unusual for the chief executive officer of a company to make over 50 behavioral deviations per week with this measurement approach when first started. We know of one chief executive officer who posted on his door his level of behavioral compliance. He reasoning was that if he is committed to change his behaviors, the rest of the organization would be willing to follow his lead.

When you have collected these four types of information and understand them, you are in a position to design a new transformation plan directed at improving morale and resiliency. Now we will agree that the average transformation plan is designed to bring about significant changes in employee morale, but some plans are also directly applied to improving resiliency as well as morale.

TYPICAL LIFE CYCLES FOR PRODUCTS AND PROJECTS

Innovative Process Phases

1. Identify
2. Create
3. Value proposition
4. Pilot
5. Business case
6. Documentation
7. Production
8. Marketing and sales
9. After-sales services
10. Evaluation results

Project Life Cycle

1. Concept exploration and definition
2. Documentation and validation
3. Engineering and manufacturing development
4. Production and deployment
5. Operations and support

Product Life Cycle

1. Concept and definition
2. Design and development
3. Creating the product service
4. Installation
5. Operations and maintenance
6. Disposal

Project Management Life Cycle

1. Concept and definition
2. Design and development
3. Creating the product or service
4. Installation

5. Operations and maintenance
6. Disposal

MURPHY'S LAWS RELATED TO ICM

There are a number of Murphy's Laws that can be applied directly to ICM:

- Nothing is as easy as it looks.
- Everything takes longer than you think.
- If anything can go wrong, it will.
- A day without crisis is a total loss.
- Inside every large problem is a series of small problems struggling to get out.
- The other line always moves faster.
- Whatever hits the fan will not be evenly distributed.
- Any tool dropped while repairing a car will roll underneath the exact center.
- Friends come and go, but enemies accumulate.
- The repairman will never have seen a model quite like yours before.
- The light at the end of the tunnel is the headlamp of an oncoming train.
- Beauty is only skin deep, but ugly goes clear to the bone.
- Murphy was an optimist.

Want to help others change? Try starting with yourself.
The best helping hand I ever got was at the end of my own arm.

BILLY ARCEMENT'S INPUTS

The following is an excerpt from Billy Arcement's June 2004 newsletter:

We've all heard people say (or perhaps you've even said it), I'm going to change my spouse, friend, enemy or employee. The truth is you cannot change anyone unless they are a willing participant.

Forget changing others. Start working on yourself. Begin thinking differently about the individual. Focus on developing a caring, non-biased, and forgiving attitude. Forget past transgressions that may have occurred and concentrate on what you want to happen in the future. Talk to the individual and share your efforts and sincerely ask them to undertake a similar mindset about you. Establish a periodic discussion time to share your personal observations regarding where the relationship is moving. Candid exchanges are the only way to make progress. There is power in one-on-one exchanges that broadens the opportunity for success.

If both parties are willing participants, positive change can and will occur. But a most important part is to have everyone "Let Go" of the past. You cannot saw sawdust so quit rehashing old wounds. The resolution is to behave differently in the future.

There is a bit of a risk here but if you sincerely feel that unless change occurs the relationship is doomed to fail, you really have nothing to risk by trying this approach because failure is eminent without change occurring.

There is within each of us a hidden power that surfaces whenever we need a boost of energy to overcome life's obstacles. It's a four-letter word, but a good one. We call it HOPE.

Hope is the magic motivator that keeps our dreams alive and our attitude positive. It is the driver of the human spirit, a builder of dreams. But the dark side of hope is often where we plant ourselves. It's called HOPELESSNESS. When we succumb to the weight of hopelessness, we give up on our dreams. We discourage all personal initiatives.

The beauty of life is that we are always free to make the choice to turn hopelessness into hope. Each day we can choose to become better, stronger and more productive individuals.

What choice will you make—hope or hopelessness?

Nothing of any great consequence has been accomplished without discipline and a will to change or improve.

Billy Arcement

The 'good old days' was last Friday and now it is Monday and the rules have changed.

H. J. Harrington

Section II

Management Action

4

Leading by Example

EXECUTIVE LEADERSHIP

> My grandmother taught me that if you want to bring about change in an organization, do it like sweeping the stairs. She said, "Always start at the top and sweep down."
>
> **H. J. Harrington**

I call it a "waterfall effect." You cannot start at the bottom of the cliff and think that the water will flow up to the top. The water (change initiative) starts at the top of the cliff and naturally flows down to the pool, often bouncing off of many rocks and cliffs (management) along the way. Can it be done? Yes, if you have a big pump and lots of power, you can reverse the flow, but that can be very costly and serves as only a temporary condition. Unfortunately, when you try to climb the falls against the flow of water, you either get pushed back or drown.

In Section I of this text, we pointed out on a number of occasions how important it was to have the key executives and managers sponsoring and being actively involved in any change initiative. Typically, in most organizations, someone steps up to the plate and assumes the role of the specific improvement champion. His or her first task is to convince an "initiating sponsor" (someone who can authorize the expenditure of the resources required to complete the project) that the improvement activity is one for which the initiating sponsor is willing to provide the required resources and invest his or her personal time. Up until the time the improvement champion has a committed initiating sponsor, there are little or no resources available to work on the activity. Often, this requires the champion to develop the sales package that will be used to convince a high-level executive that the project is of sufficient value to justify him or her serving as the initiating sponsor.

As you can see, the start of all improvement and new product processes starts with a very high-level manager authorizing the resources to evaluate and install specific activity.

Why Managers First

Why start with managers? The answers are simple if you just look at their areas of responsibility. Managers are responsible for the following:

- Allocating resources
- Establishing the organization's structure
- Selecting the leaders
- Developing the processes
- Setting performance standards
- Making job assignments
- Preparing the job description
- Providing the measurement and reward systems
- Setting priorities
- Selecting and training employees

Considering management's responsibilities, it is obvious that first we must execute these responsibilities in a superior manner if we hope to succeed in the activity. Only when management executes their responsibilities can we hope to release the enthusiasm and pent-up creativity that exist in our employees.

When managers were employees, they got the word through the grapevine. Then when they were promoted into management, they thought they were being promoted into the inner sanctum. They thought that they would be provided with all the inside data, but in most cases, that is not true. Top management considers middle and first-line managers as the employees' representatives, so they are not allowed to share in the organization's critical information because upper management fears that it will be disseminated to the employees. On the other end of the spectrum, they are quickly dropped from the rumor mill because they represent management, and, of course, they already know. The result is that an information void is created. One manager shared his concerns with me, stating, "I find out more about what's going on in the organization by reading *The Wall Street Journal* at lunch than I do at all of our staff meetings."

Even Japanese firms do not involve middle management in their decisions when they are operating outside of Japan. In a survey conducted by the Japanese Machinery Export Association on Japanese companies doing business in Western Europe, 67% of the 94 companies participating in the survey stated that they are unwilling to let locally hired staff take part in decisions on raising funds for long-term purposes. Seventy-six percent stated that locally hired staff should not be permitted to have a voice in making decisions on new plants. Forty-two percent said that they are unwilling to allow local staff to take part in research and development. Nobuhiko Kawamoto, when he was president of Honda Corporation, stopped using Japanese-style consensus management in his U.S. operations in preference to an American-type organization chart. As a result, communication and decision making have become much faster within the modern Honda Corporation.

Management Leadership

I have worked in the business environment for over 47 years, and I have yet to find one manager who performs at an equivalent quality level to the average production worker. A good production worker consistently performs at the parts-per-million error level. Most managers perform at the errors-per-hundred level: Missed schedules. Starting meetings late. Not following up on commitments. Lack of prompt feedback. The list of management errors goes on and on. Why do we live with these gross management errors? We believe it is because no one takes the time to prepare a management activity inspection plan and conduct audits of management's performance similar to those that are conducted in the manufacturing operations. We set low expectations of our managers. We just do not expect management to perform at the parts-per-million level. We have grown to accept mediocrity and superior management performance. The biggest single opportunity for improvement in business today is management performance.

The following are the major roadblocks to improvement within most organizations:

- Lack of employee trust
- Lack of management credibility
- Lack of training
- Poor communication
- Fear of risk-taking
- Lack of delegation
- Untimely decision-making

- Misdirected measurements systems
- Lack of employee loyalty
- Lack of continuity

Each of these roadblocks can only be broken down by management. Without the removal of these roadblocks, the organization cannot make major progress. For example, we have learned from the many surveys we have conducted that the single area that is most often rated as the one that needs to be improved first by the employee is *trust in management.*

You can buy employees' time, effort, and skills, but you cannot buy their enthusiasm, loyalty, and trust. These must be earned by management. Salary increases and bonuses will not do it. Only a close, open, honest, personal relationship between management and the employee will do it. It is a two-way street that must be started by management respecting and trusting their employees. Too often, management gets quickly disappointed when they cast their bread on the water and do not see it immediately returned. This is a process that management has to prime many times to overcome the negative feelings they have built up in our employees in the past. It requires that management develop a true and sincere interest in their employees, not just as providers of services, but also as individuals with problems, personal needs, families, and concerns. Too many managers today believe that loyalty is dead and that employees only care about "what's in it for me."

Management's actions over the past decade have certainly dampened employees' spirits and increased their distrust of management's loyalty to them. You can't pick up a newspaper without seeing articles about employee layoffs, government cutbacks, and organizations requesting that their employees put forth additional effort with less and less resources. In reality, loyalty and trust are down because management has driven them down. This reflects the frustration that employees have with management who hasn't bothered to truly take an interest in developing close personal relationships with employees and to take personal responsibility for them. This distant style of management is the result of an inner sense that if they keep the employees at arm's length and something negative happens within the organization, management won't feel so bad about laying them off. Management needs to truly demonstrate that they are concerned about their employees, not just their own interests. Most employees want to trust management and be loyal to the organization, but they have been given little reason to do so.

As managers, we have to deserve their trust and loyalty by our actions. We earn their trust and loyalty by being sincerely and genuinely interested in the employees' present and future goals, by appreciating their viewpoints and helping them reach their career goals, and by dealing with them as adults and providing them with information so that they can make intelligent decisions. Building trust and loyalty is difficult in today's environment, but it can be done and is being done by managers who are truly interested in their people. Those managers that take time and make the effort find that it is well worth the price they pay.

Management has destroyed its own credibility often without knowing or understanding why. Typical mistakes that management makes that destroy credibility are as follows:

- Hiding bad news from employees
- Saying half-truths or outright lying
- Not living up to the mission, values, and visions
- Not taking action on poor performers
- Dodging decisions

Credibility builds trust. Trust builds loyalty. Loyalty breeds success not only for the individual, but also for the organization as a whole. This important cycle has to start with management and is a key function before we call on the employee to start to improve.

Why Top Management Keeps ICM at Arm's Length

Too often we approach management and ask for their support of the improvement process based on intangibles. We explain that it will improve customer satisfaction, reduce waste, or improve morale. This approach gets their support, gets them saying "Hallelujah!", but does not get them up in the pulpit preaching or out working with the congregation. What we need to do is provide top management with tangible data that prove the business case for implementing the ICM process. Some of the best ways to convince management that they should support and actively lead the ICM process efforts are

1. Competitive benchmarking
2. Market studies
3. Customer surveys/focus groups
4. Cost analysis

5. Improvement-needs analysis
6. Customer-loss analysis

It is important at the start to clearly define why the organization needs to improve. It should not be because another organization is doing it or to improve employee morale. It should be one or more of the following:

- Get a "bigger piece of the pie" (increase market share)
- Create a "bigger pie" for everyone
- Improve the bottom line
- Ensure long-term survival and growth
- Increase job security
- Combat competitive pressure

MANAGEMENT'S ROLE

These are specific roles that management at all levels must play in the improvement process. These roles clearly demonstrate a very participative environment down to the point that the employee teams are granted the right of developing their own work processes. In this approach, the strategic plan provides the guidance, not the control of the process.

The following is a list of requirements for employee involvement and participative management to thrive within the work environment:

1. Management will have to share the power and responsibility.
2. Management must provide the employees with much more information than they have in the past.
3. Participative management/employee involvement needs to be practiced at all levels of management.
4. Management needs to trust their employees in order to earn the trust of their employees.
5. Management needs to feel comfortable with decentralized decision-making.
6. Management needs to stop performing hindsight appraisals.
7. Management must encourage an environment where failures are accepted as being part of the learning cycle, and risk-taking is a dominant trait of the people who get ahead.

8. Time must be made available to train the employees in how to make decisions, learn new jobs, and perform business analysis.
9. Management must have the courage to reject poor solutions but take time to explain why the suggestion is being rejected.

For an organization to be successful, management must provide employees with

1. Detailed job descriptions
2. Relevant measures that can be used to evaluate progress
3. Tools so that the employees can perform error-free work
4. Job-related training so that employees understand how to use the tools and the processes that management provides
5. An understanding of the importance of the job and why it is being performed
6. Ongoing, continuous customer feedback so that employees can evaluate their performance
7. Time to do the job correctly

Basic Beliefs

The sophisticated management methods rely on some basic beliefs that must be mastered before these methods can be applied. Managers who have not mastered these basic beliefs stand a major exposure to being the individuals that are left out in the cold during the next restructuring cycle. These basic beliefs are as follows:

- *Delegation.* Management must be able to accomplish assignments by delegating work to their direct reports. Management must be able to free itself to do planning, break down barriers, teach, measure, and network.
- *Appraisal.* Management must be able to develop individual performance goals in cooperation with the employee, and must provide honest, continuous feedback on performance compared to their goals.
- *Disagreement.* Disagreements between management and employees can be healthy. Management needs to understand both sides of the situation to make the very best decision. "Yes"-type men or women are not helpful.

- *Be decisive.* Management cannot be reluctant to make a decision. Often, "gut feeling" is an extremely important part of managing the organization.
- *Positive attitude.* If the manager conveys a feeling of failure, the department is doomed to defeat.
- *Five-way communication system.* Management must establish excellent upward, downward, sideways, supplier, and customer communication systems. They must be willing to share information with their employees. Information is power. Every year, Robert Crandall, chief executive officer of American Airlines, conducts 20–30 President's Conferences in his 165-city route system, ensuring he maintains open communication with all of his employees.
- *Invest.* Management should invest heavily in its employees, provide them with training, and help them grow and mature. This is one of the best investments an organization can make. Art Wegner, chief executive officer of Pratt Whitney Turbo Manufacturing, sent his design engineers into the plant to spend 6 months on assignment as general foremen. Certainly, this is a major investment in their future, but it has paid off in improved manufacturability of new products designed by these engineers.

Overcontrolled and Under-Led

Management talks participation and empowerment, but in today's environment with organizational flattening, more and more, instead of less and less, decisions are being made by higher and higher levels of management. These negative trends need to stop, and the best way to stop them is for each level of management to question each decision they make to be sure they should be making it. If the decision could be made at a lower level, the decision should be directed to the proper individual. We realize that at first this may slow down the process even further, but people soon get the word, and only the proper level of decisions will be escalated up the management ladder. In addition, management cannot second-guess decisions that are made.

Improvement's Negative Impact on Management

The improvement efforts going on in Western countries have hit management extremely hard. Most organizations are trying to flatten their organizational structures by eliminating middle managers. In a survey of 836 organizations conducted by the American Management Association last year, middle management made up 5% of the workforce, but accounted for 22% of the past year's layoffs. Lower-level managers are beginning to feel the impact of self-managed work teams. Unfortunately, when we lose our managers, we are losing the cream of our employees. In most cases we selected them because they were the most productive, most technically competent individuals in the group. We have invested vast sums of time, effort, and money in further developing their skills. They should be our very best employees. If they are not, it is not their fault, for at some point in time they were the best.

If we accept the reality that most organizations have a smaller span of control than they need, it is inevitable that some managers must go. Management needs to find a way to decrease the number of managers without losing this valuable resource and without embarrassing the individual. The answer to this dilemma is to establish a dual growth ladder combined with a management technical vitality program.

Many organizations talk about a dual growth ladder. One side is for management skills, and the other is for technical expertise. This approach has the advantage that superior technical people need not transfer into management and become poor managers to have a growth path within the organization. It also allows managers to move back and forth freely into technical roles without being unduly or unfairly impacted. The dual ladder also provides an excellent solution to the organization's problem of management technical vitality. Today, a manager who moves out of management is looked at by the total organization as a failure. As a result, managers dogmatically use all their skills and contacts to hide their obsolete technical competence to stay in management. They work excessive hours to look good in front of other managers and misuse the time of the employees that report to keep them informed and explain what they are doing.

A technical vitality program for middle management will solve most of these problems. Many organizations have started to rotate their middle managers into technical assignments for 3 years, after being in management for 6 years. No manager is exempt from this rotation. Every middle manager knows that every 6 years he or she will be placed in a technical vitality assignment, so there is no shame associated with rotating out of management. The organization benefits as soon as the rotation project starts because they automatically can reduce the number of middle managers by one-third. The organization also benefits when the middle manager returns from the technical vitality assignment, because he or she has a better understanding of the technical side of business. This truly is a win-win activity for middle management and the organization.

Tomorrow's Managers

The term "management" should be treated as a set of concepts, not as a group of people. Traditional management, as we know it today, has evolved as follows:

- Individualistic management
- Professional management
- Scientific management
- Human relations management
- Participative management

> Certainly I'm not in a position to lead unless I really understand the (improvement process) concept really well. That's why I read a lot of books and went to a lot of seminars.
>
> **Steve Moksnes**
> *President of AccuRate*

In the nineteenth century, the management style could have been called, "Individualistic Management." The entrepreneur was responsible for creating most of the large organizations that we have today. Families like the Fords, Rockefellers, Carnegies, DuPonts, Sloans, and Watsons were all creative individualists who built and managed great organizations. This approach, driven by the economics of business, gave way to the Professional Management era, where management was measured by the short-term bottom line. The professional manager's goal was to produce the maximum output with the minimum expenditure.

This led naturally into Frederick Winslow Taylor's scientific management approach to running an organization. Scientific management was based on four principles:

1. Scientifically designing the job.
2. Scientifically selecting workers to match the job requirements.
3. Scientifically training the workers to perform the job as designed.
4. Doing the work in a spirit of cooperation.

This worked well with workers who had low skill level and low intelligence. This approach divided the work process into small assignments that required little training. As management's style became more and more autocratic and the employee became better educated, the system began to break down. The employees began to resent management who, from the employee's standpoint, were taking advantage of them. As a result, "Human Relations Management" became the preferred management system. Human relations management is based on the belief that if management treats the employee with respect and dignity, the employee's performance will be maximized—a simple idea for a simple situation. Unfortunately, today's working environment is anything but simple. As a result, the management style of the future must be a "Participative Management" style.

Tomorrow's managers will have to be much more effective than they are today. They will have a much bigger span of control or, as I like to think of it, a larger span of support and new, more demanding challenges. They will become more and more impacted with the soft side of management, since most technical decisions will be made by intelligent computers. As employees become empowered to be responsible and accountable for their jobs, management's role must change. Table 4.1 shows how the management's environment at all levels is and will be changing.

Job Descriptions

The job description is the way most organizations define and communicate the form, fit, and function of each job and define its value to the organization. Each assignment is guided based on the job description. In many organizations, job descriptions have proliferated to the point that they are dragging the organization down. Often, in these and other organizations, job descriptions are out of date and, as a result, not usable. The basic objective behind the job description approach to designing and evaluating jobs is a sound one, but now we need to make it a value-added tool. In some cases when job descriptions are poorly written, employees can use them to get out of doing a specific job. For example, the drilling

TABLE 4.1

Management Is Changing

Activity	Yesterday	Today	Tomorrow
Management style	Dictating	Coaching	Assisting
Providing direction	Orders	Consensus	Define results
Goal setting	Management's goals	Common goals	Employee evaluations
Decision-making	Management decisions	Team decisions	Individual decisions
Compensation	Pay for years worked	Pay for performance	Pay for knowledge
Way to correct problems	Focus on individual	Focus on activity	Focus on progress

machine operator may take a position that the job description does not indicate that he is responsible for sweeping up the chips in his work area. Typically, the job description should be written by the manager of the individual who is doing that job. Normally, personnel will refine it to be sure that there are no misunderstandings related to the work that needs to be accomplished.

- Manager's job description
  Frequently, management job descriptions are out of date and currently not in keeping with the new improvement environment. The typical manager's job described is written for directors, the people who "kick ass" and make things happen. Frequently, the whole social side of management is completely ignored. Often there is no requirement in the job description for the manager to develop his or her employees. One of the very first steps in implementing the innovative concepts has to be restructuring the manager's job description so that it is in line with expected management performance. These management job descriptions should be divided into three major sections. They are
  - Technical
  - Business management
  - Employee development

    See the need and take the lead.

    H. J. Harrington

- Employees' job descriptions
  Equally as important as the manager's job description is the employee's job description. In an environment where we are empowering the employees to make all appropriate decisions related to their job, their job description soon becomes obsolete. As a result, management needs to go back and rewrite job descriptions so that they reflect the increased innovative responsibility placed on the individual. Then the job should be reevaluated to determine if the employee is getting a fair day's pay for a fair day's work. It is important to minimize the number of job description levels associated with pay ranges. This allows and encourages the employees to move from one assignment to another, increasing their knowledge and experience base while increasing their value to the organization. The use of job rotation

programs helps keep morale high when there are few promotional opportunities available within an organization.

The following is a typical innovative statement that would be included in the job description:

> This assignment requires the individual to make use of his/her physical and mental capabilities to identify and implement (when possible) value-identifying improvement opportunities and develop creative solutions for them and the ones that the organization faces on a day-to-day basis.

5

The Innovative Manager

MANAGERS ARE ULTIMATELY HELD ACCOUNTABLE

When all is said and done, the management team is held responsible for the organization's performance. How well the organization performs is directly reflected in their promotions, salaries, and longevity with the organization. In this country, management's exposures are limited to reduced salary or loss of position. In China, poor performance is dealt with in a much more hostile manner. The Minister of Economic China, Reform spokesman, Xi Ten Huan, said, "It is understandable our citizens would express shock and outrage when managers are careless in their attitudes towards the welfare of others." China is not the only country that holds its managers accountable. Russia feels the same way about its managers.

We are not recommending these types of stern actions on the U.S. government's part, but it is time that management steps up to their responsibility to improve the quality, reliability, and productivity of our organizations.

If our management team is going to be held accountable for the improvement, then they must be involved in the implementation of any improvement process. This involvement must extend far beyond knowledge of its existence. They must become the leaders of the movement. They must be the shakers, the movers, and the teachers. If our employees are to excel, then our management must excel. As someone once said, "We are what we repeatedly do. Excellence, then, is not an act. It is a habit."

HOW TO GET CREATIVITY, INNOVATION, INVOLVEMENT, AND PARTICIPATIVE MANAGEMENT TO THRIVE

The following is a list of requirements for employee innovation, involvement, and participative management to thrive within the work environment:

1. Management will have to share the power and responsibility.
2. Management must provide the employees with much more information than they have in the past.
3. Participative management/employee involvement needs to be practiced at all levels of management.
4. Management needs to trust their employees in order to earn the trust of all the employees.
5. Management needs to feel comfortable with decentralized decision-making.
6. Management needs to stop performing hindsight appraisals.
7. Management must encourage an environment where failures are accepted as being part of the learning cycle and risk-taking is a dominant trait of the people who get ahead.
8. Time must be made available to train the employees in how to make decisions, learn new jobs, and perform business analysis.
9. Management must have the courage to reject poor solutions, but take time to explain why the suggestion is being rejected.

Things Successful Managers Must Do

For an organization to be successful, management must provide employees with

1. Detailed job descriptions
2. Relevant measures that can be used to evaluate progress
3. Tools so that the employees can perform error-free work
4. Job-related training so that employees understand how to use the tools and the processes that management provides
5. An understanding of the importance of the job and why it is being performed

6. Ongoing, continuous customer feedback so that employees can evaluate their performance
7. Time to do the job correctly

Caught in the Middle

Let's be honest with ourselves. Middle and first-line managers have been caught up in a pressure cooker as the country presses for flatter organizations, and programs like self-managed work teams become a way of life. In the 1980s, managers made up 10% of the U.S. industrial workforce. Organizations like AT&T had more than 100 layers of management. Certainly, they were prime candidates for job elimination. Management guru Peter F. Drucker stated, "The cynicism out there is frightening. Middle managers have become insecure, and they feel unbelievably hurt. They feel like slaves on an auction block" (Resource Management Excellence, Paton Press, 2007, p. 187). Organizations like IBM, General Motors, Westinghouse, General Electric, Mobil, Ford, and DuPont have slashed their management ranks. Management jobs have been combined, creating what we originally thought would be more meaningful and challenging work. Instead we have created an atmosphere where managers feel overburdened and underappreciated.

Yes, middle and first-level managers are very unsure of their status in most organizations today. The probability of being let go is much higher than the probability of promotion. Their futures have been put on hold and their life savings are in jeopardy. It is absolutely imperative that we do not skip over them and go directly to our employees, or we will lose their support. The early retirement programs that most organizations implemented in the late 1980s and early 1990s have allowed the most talented, most knowledgeable managers to escape the organization. We cannot further alienate the managers we have.

It is often necessary to get rid of managers who are not well-rounded. In one organization where we were asked to redesign the organization structure to make it more customer centric, over one-third of the managers were classified as surplus. Two levels of management were dropped, and the communication system was greatly strengthened. With so many surplus managers, how do you select the right ones to stay in management? What we did was develop career plans for each of the managers. Many of the managers we talked to were technically extremely capable but did not like the business aspects and the employee development part of the management assignment. Many of them accepted the managerial job only because it was the only promotional career path available to them. Once we established a dual career path up through the plant manager level that had the same prestige that the managers received, we had a number of managers volunteer to step into technical roles.

Most managers who have less than five people reporting to them do not have a full-time management job. They take their spare time and dedicate it to the technical side of the managerial assignment. Because they enjoy the technical side more than the business or personal development side of the job assignment, the business and personal development side slips to do the technical side of the operation. As a result, the business and personal development side of the responsibility does not get done, and another manager is added to correct the problem. Of course, this just compounds the problem as the new manager discovers he or she has even more time to work on the technical parts of the assignment.

Employment Security

As you will note, we started discussing employee security in Section I of this book. We have decided to continue and reemphasize it in Section II because it is such a prominent deterrent to organizational change. Employment security is one of the most critical and complex political and economic issues facing top management as a result of foreign competition, outsourcing, and improvement initiatives that have been initiated within most organizations.

Management must determine the following:

- Is the employee an investment or a cost?
- How much improved performance and flexibility would be generated if the organization provided employment security?
- Is it better to retain or relocate employees or hire new ones?
- Should the organization look at other ways of handling surplus employees besides layoffs?

The employee must determine the following:

- What impact will the organization's change initiatives have on my employment security?

- Will the organization's change activities jeopardize or improve my standard of living?
- Would I be willing to change jobs or move to another location?
- Will I be more valuable as a result of what I'm learning during the change process?

How can we expect our employees to give freely of their ideas to increase their productivity and minimize waste if it means that their job or the job of their friends will be eliminated? If you start a continuous improvement process and then have layoffs, what you are going to end up with is a continuous sabotage process.

Corporate America has been on a downsizing kick since the late 1980s. Its answer to business pressure is to slow down and lay off workers, with the hope of rising stock prices, but that does not work. In an analysis published by *U.S. News & World Report,* the stock prices of organizations that went through a major downsizing in the last half of the 1980s were compared with those within the industry group. On average, the organizations that downsized saw a 10% improvement in stock prices over the first 6 months after the downsizing occurred. Six months later, stock values went negative by about 1%. Three years after the downsizing, they were negative on average of 25%

Layoffs produce sudden, substantial stock gains. These gains occur because the impact of removed employees has not reached the customer and the competition has not been removed from the bottom line, making organizations appear to be more profitable than they really are. But in the long run, the downsizing had a negative impact. Ex-Chief Executive Officer (CEO) Frank Popoff of Dow Chemical put it this way, "Layoffs are horribly expensive and destructive of shareholder value" (Change Management, CRC Press, 2016, p. 348).

The cost of layoffs and replacement is growing all the time. Dow Chemical estimates that it costs $30,000 to $100,000 to replace technical- and managerial-type personnel. Layoffs not only cost organizations money and some of its best people, but when it comes time to hire, the best people do not trust the organization and will not come to work for them.

An alternative approach of a golden parachute or early retirement is equally bad. The people who leave are all the best performers who will not have problems finding a new job. The deadwood, who barely meet minimum performance, stay because they know it will be hard to find an equally good job in today's job market.

Employees can understand that organizations need to cut back when demand for their products falls off, and they can accept that. The problem we face is what happens to an employee whose job has been eliminated due to an improvement initiative? We know that programs like Six Sigma, lean, and reengineering are designed to improve productivity. But if our share of the market does not keep pace with our productivity improvements, what will management do with surplus employees? To cover this scenario and to alleviate employee fears, top management should release a "no layoff policy." A typical no layoff policy would state:

> No employee will be laid off because of improvements made as a result of the change process going on within the organization. People whose jobs are eliminated will be retrained for an equally or more responsible job. This does not mean that it may not be necessary to lay off employees because of a business turndown.

You will note that the policy does not guarantee the employees will not be laid off as a result of a turndown in business. It only protects the employees from being laid off as a result of the change initiative. These are people who would still be working for the organization if the change initiative had not been implemented.

We know of one organization that was able to eliminate 203 jobs as a result of their change initiatives. As they started their change initiatives, they put a freeze on new hiring and used temporary employees to cover workload peaks. This was reviewed with the labor union leaders, and they concurred with the use of temporary employees to protect regular employees' jobs. As a result, attrition took care of about 80 surplus jobs. The organization then held a contest to select 62 employees who were sent to a local university to work toward an engineering degree. While at school, they received full pay and their additional expenses were paid for by the organization. The results were phenomenal. Everyone within the organization started looking for ways to eliminate their job so they could go to school.

Trust and Confidence

It is important to build a competent, close-working team that performs both efficiently and effectively without stifling the creativity of the individual. This requires that every member on the team trust and understand each other. Management needs to trust its employees and share the power that information about the organization provides to everyone. In the past, management spoon-fed employees with only enough data to do their job, holding back most of the key operational information. This builds a false sense of power for management and fosters a feeling of distrust in the employee. Providing everyone with as much data as possible is always best, because it short-circuits the rumor mill that acts something like this:

- Unknown (first person)—John tells Mary: "I think there could be a layoff." "I don't know if there will be a layoff or not."
- Rumor (second person)—Mary tells Ruth: "We could have as many as 1000 employees laid off."
- Fact (third person)—Ruth tells Harry: "There will be 1000 employees laid off next month."
- Results (fourth person)—Harry tells John: "They are going to lay off 1000 people next month. I have started looking for a new job. How about you?" John says, "I am going to get out of here before the market gets flooded with people from this company."

As the Old Testament states, "People perish from lack of knowledge." To earn trust and understanding from their employees, management must provide them with a secure environment. Management must realize that any improvement process will cause the employees to ask themselves the following questions:

- What is in it for me if I make the organization more productive?
- Will productivity improvements cost me my job or reduce my standard of living?
- Am I willing to change jobs or relocate to stay with the organization?
- What will my future be with the organization?

These are known as "silent questions" that management must help the employee answer to provide a secure environment. This can best be accomplished by management's positive actions, not words.

Tell Them Why

Everyone wants to have self-respect and to be respected by others. This is a universal need that we all have, and it's a need management needs to fulfill more today than ever before. For without self-respect, it is impossible to build trust and loyalty. Showing that you respect a person is a sincere form of flattery. Think of how you handle people. The higher level a person is, the more you respect him or her, the more time you take to explain why you are doing something. When you do not feel a person is important, you have the tendency to tell that person what to do. You tell your children to take out the garbage or to do the dishes. The more you respect an individual, the more time you take to explain why they should do something. Management often falls into this trap of telling their employees what to do without explaining why it is worth their time and effort to do it. It is always better to tell employees why they need to do something in preference to how to do it.

A boss tells an employee how to do something. The modern manager tells the employee why it needs to be done, taking the manager out of the role of boss and putting him in the role of a modern leader and associate. No longer are you ordering employees to do something. You are helping them to understand the results that need to be accomplished, the impact the activity has on the organization, and a sense of urgency. Telling an employee how to do a job may get it done, but explaining why the job needs to be done gets it done with enthusiasm. People who understand why, develop their own approach for accomplishing the task, make fewer errors, and complete the assignment faster because they have a sense of ownership. They will also feel free to change their approach as the situation changes. If employees do not understand why they are doing the task, the charge ahead is implementing management's direction until they are stopped.

Do It with a Smile

A smile goes a mile, while a frown drives you down. A smile unlocks the door of acceptance. It denotes friendship, caring, and a willingness to listen to both sides of the story. Managers who have a smile on their face, a twinkle in their eye, and sincerity in their voice, breed an environment of friendship and cooperation into the entire workplace—the energy level of the total department surges. People like to work for managers who are friendly, likable, and have a positive attitude. Too often under the pressures of the job, managers forget that everyone looks to them to set the attitude of the organization. Other managers think that they won't be taken seriously if they don't appear to be a little aloof, firm, and stern. They rely on the harsh personality to give them stature and respect. But that's not true. Sure, you can get short-term results by threatening people, but you build long-term team relationships and performance by creating an enjoyable work environment.

People just perform better when they are happy and satisfied with their job, when they are not threatened by their job and their manager. What are the key management characteristics that make a work environment enjoyable?

- Sincere interest in the employee
- Easy to talk with
- Treats everyone as equally important
- Comfortable to be around
- Friendly and pleasant personality
- Not above doing any job
- Realizes that other people are busy, too
- Does not bring personal problems to work
- Has a consistent personality that can be depended on
- Remembers commitments
- Shares success and shoulders blame

President Dwight D. Eisenhower typified this type of person. There was never any doubt that he was in command and meant what he said, but he always had a smile for everyone. Although a smile or a frown can make management convincing, it is meaning what you say and following through to be sure it is accomplished that really counts.

Listening

As managers, we need to be good listeners. We were born with two ears and only one mouth. I believe this is a sign that we should listen twice as much as we talk. Our employees cannot tell us what their problems are or what they are thinking when we are talking. Make effective use of silence to encourage your employees to talk. Take the time to develop good listening habits. Some useful guidelines are as follows:

- Gather as many ideas as possible before making a decision
- Look directly at the person who is talking to you
- Use words of encouragement like: "Yes, I understand, tell me more."
- Put your phone on hold when someone comes in to talk to you.
- Ask probing questions, and do not jump to conclusions.
- Take time to chat with coworkers.
- Ration the time you talk.
- Understand what is behind their words.
- Listen with your eyes and ears.

Urgency and Persistence

Today's work environment is very fast moving, and management must create a sense of urgency in every employee's mind. People who make things happen radiate energy and a sense of urgency. A good manager is a person who does not put off until tomorrow anything that someone can be made to do today. The world is full of good intentions. Many well-meaning, brilliant people turn out to be unsuccessful because they have made it a habit of putting things off until tomorrow—people who do not start working on a project until it is almost due, and then something interrupts them so that they miss the schedule. Success comes to the manager who makes things happen on schedule without sacrificing quality or cost. The quality of that last-minute job is usually compromised. Good managers know how to communicate a sense of urgency without being obnoxious and overbearing. They do it by showing interest, by reviewing plans, by checking progress, and by being there to help break down the roadblocks that get in the way of their employees. There is no substitute for management interest. The things that management is interested in get done. The other things may or may not get done.

The combination of urgency and persistence makes a winning formula for management and employees alike. As important as a sense of urgency is, it takes persistence to get the job done. Calvin Coolidge put it this way, "Nothing in the world can take the place of persistence. Talent will not: Nothing is more common than unsuccessful people with talent. Genius will not: Unrewarded genius is almost a proverb. Education will not: The world is full of educated derelicts. Persistence and determination alone are omnipotent. The slogan 'press on' has solved and always will solve the problems of the human race" (Resource Management Excellence, Paton Press, 2007, p. 29).

RECOGNIZING GOOD AND BAD PERFORMANCE—THE FEEDBACK PROCESS

Most people want to do a good job and feel that they are contributing to the success of the organization. Today's manager must provide ongoing, continuous feedback on both the negative and positive aspects of performance. If the employee's manager does not pay close attention to the employee's output, it is perceived as not being of value. So the employee reasons: What difference does it make how good or how bad the job is done? Employees who rarely receive feedback feel that their job is unimportant and that no one cares. And if all they receive is negative feedback, they feel that they are inadequate and that management is down on them.

Use positive feedback to reinforce desired behavior patterns. Things like when the employee goes out of his or her way to help other employees, comes up with unique ideas, beats schedules, handles difficult situations, catches an error, puts out additional effort, or sacrifices self-interest for the sake of the assignment. The best positive feedback occurs in public, at a meeting, on a bulletin board, with a group of associates, and so on. At times, it is best to send a personal note to provide private feedback. But do not wait. It always is best to provide positive and negative feedback as close to the time that the activity occurs as possible.

Most managers find it difficult to give negative feedback but feel it is the primary reason that they have their job. As a result, they charge into it like a bull in a china closet, trying to get it over with as soon as possible. But it is important to realize that people are a lot like magnets: They are drawn by positives and repelled by negatives. The challenge for management today is to provide negative feedback in a constructive way. Management must talk results, not about the individual's personal attitudes or actions. They must probe deeply into the employee's side of the situation so they thoroughly understand the circumstances surrounding the incident. They should couch the criticism in a way that allows the employees to save face. The manager is not there to win the battle. His or her job is to try and help the employees change bad attitudes or approaches to their assignments. Remember, you can effectively make your point without nailing the employee to the cross.

PARTICIPATION/EMPLOYEE INVOLVEMENT

Participation, empowerment, and employee involvement—all are current buzzwords today, but these are words that bring about a cold chill to the heart of the bravest middle and first-level manager. Theoretically, and even outwardly, these programs are usually supported by middle management, because upper management wants them done now. But down inside, middle managers interpret them as ways to eliminate their jobs. In the massive layoffs that have occurred, middle and first-level managers have taken the biggest percentage of the burden. In this environment of career uncertainty, how do you think managers feel about employee involvement?

With middle and first-level managers' deep concerns about participative management and employee involvement, how can you expect the processes to work? Can top management edict it into the organization? Yes. Can they edict it into the organization and will it work? No. Our middle and first-level managers are too wise to outwardly buck top management when they tell them that they want to install a participative management process. The middle managers think that they are not involved, that it's the first-level managers who have to do it. The first-level managers get the word that top management wants them to give up some of their responsibilities to their employees. The word spreads like wildfire that this is the start of self-managed work teams—an environment where the first-level managers' jobs are eliminated. The first-level managers cooperate because the top of the organization tells them they have to. Both middle and first-level managers must be more participative, but they do not change themselves, nor do they require middle management to change. Isn't there something wrong with this process? Yes, the process is flawed, and it can lead to spending a lot of money on training and nonproductive meetings.

When participative management is implemented correctly, it starts with top management. But, instead of giving orders, they give up some of their responsibility to middle management. Typically, they give up the month-to-month firefighting activities that take so much of their time. This creates a heavy workload for middle management, who already is overworked, causing them to delegate more of their work to the first-level manager. As first-level managers become more empowered, and have fewer checks and balances to report up the ladder, they will see that upper management believes that participative management is the way of the future and is essential for their future growth. Because most people want to emulate the people whom they report to, participative management flows willingly throughout the organization. In this environment, first-level managers willingly give up some of their responsibilities to their employees and welcome the employees' contributions to the planning and decision-making processes that relate to their work assignments.

If participative management is implemented correctly, upper management has more time to do things they should have been doing all along but have never had the time because they were too busy fighting fires and worrying about the quarterly bottom line. What should upper management do with the freed-up time that participative management gives them? They should use this newly found time as follows:

- Work with employees to understand the real problems.
- Talk to the external customers to understand their present and future needs.
- Provide direction through the strategic planning process.

Marvin Runyon, CEO of Nissan Motor Manufacturing Corporation, spends time with each of his 3200 employees at least once a year. Does your CEO have time to do the same? If not, maybe he or she needs to be more participative.

Remember that participative management does not mean democratic management. The law of one person—one vote, does not apply to participative management because the managers are still held accountable for the actions of the people who report to them. Management should encourage the employees to freely contribute their ideas and empower them to implement them, but management must have the courage to reject ideas that are not the best solution for the organization. When ideas are rejected, it is very important for management to take the time to explain why the suggested solution was not the correct answer for the organization. If this feedback process is not handled very well, the idea stream will soon dry up.

The Push–Pull of Management

General Dwight Eisenhower used to show the difference between leadership styles with a piece of string. Pull it and your employees will follow you anywhere. Push it and the team goes nowhere. Managers who prod and threaten to get the job done are pushing on the end of the string. People who push on the end of the string rarely get the best performance from their employees. The employees work against management, not with them. Their only desire is to get the boss off their back. Managers who pull the other end of the string have the employees working with them. Managers help the employees to be their very best. They break down roadblocks and concentrate on making it easy for the employee to perform (see Figure 5.1).

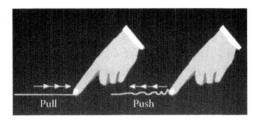

FIGURE 5.1
Impact of pushing/pulling.

How to Get Employees to Work

Management's role is to get work done through others. We must realize that the work ethic is something that has to be learned; it is not an inborn trait. Many experiments with animals and people have proven beyond a doubt that the work ethic is a learned trait. In these experiments, when individuals are provided with all their desires without doing anything to earn them, they replace their work with less productive ways of occupying their time. Unfortunately, work ethics are developed during the formative part of a person's life, between the ages of 2 and 15. By the time people enter into the adult world, their work ethics have already been formed.

As America has developed and prospered, work ethics have degraded. At the start of the nineteenth century, people lived to work. The harder you worked, the better person you were. Honest labor was a valued trait that would lead to success. As survival became a given, and government stepped in to provide a minimum living standard for everyone, work ethics began to slip.

As America became more and more successful, parents expected less and less from their children. Honest labor was replaced with time in front of the TV. Dishwashers eliminated the need for children to work with their parents when doing dishes. Product reliability improvements and increased financial wealth have reduced the need for the parents to work with the child in repairing the car, the washing machine, the plumbing, and so on. Store-bought frozen foods, cakes, bread, and so forth, have reduced the time that both the parent and the child spend in the kitchen working together. Fast food has for many families all but eliminated the need for a kitchen. This reduction in time and effort required to run the home has freed up the wife to become a very important part of today's workforce, which has led to the emancipation of women. This added freedom did not come too soon, because as male earnings dropped off, women were forced to step in and shoulder part of the financial burden. As a result, families with both partners working are the rule rather than the exception, in order to maintain their desired standards of living.

Coupling this new financial security for women with the decrease in family work projects has had a very negative impact on family values, leading to a period where a one-parent family is not unusual. The result is an ongoing decline in work values. As a result of these factors, there has been a drastic reduction in the honest work time that children are involved in. We estimate that an average 12-year-old today only works 15% of the time that a 12-year-old worked in 1940.

As society became more affluent, people began to balance their lives between the various areas that occupy their time and account for the major interest in their lives. Figure 5.2a presents the theoretical arena of life. In the past, "work" was the overriding quadrant in the arena of life, and the other three quadrants were allocated to the leftovers (Figure 5.2b). Today, work is used to make the other three quadrants possible (Figure 5.2c). The quadrant of "self" that was almost ignored in the 1950s has become more important, with ever-growing portions of the individual's time being devoted to it, as an individual spends more time staying in good physical condition and indulging in self-pleasures like watching television, attending sports activities, and listening to high-quality music.

In the 1940s and 1950s, employees used to line up to work overtime. Everyone wanted to work Saturday for time-and-a-half. Managers needed to keep very close records on the number of overtime hours each employee worked so they did not show preferences. Today, just the opposite condition exists. It is difficult to find anyone who will work overtime. Everyone

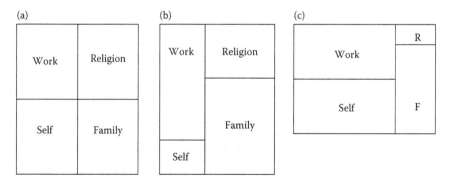

FIGURE 5.2
The arena of life (in percentage of hours awake). (a) Theoretical, (b) 1950s, and (c) 2010s.

expects 2 days' advance notice if they have to work overtime. The work quadrant today has been neatly boxed in, and the other three quadrants are jealously guarded to ensure that work does not interfere with them.

In this environment, management needs to look closely at their management style to ensure they are in tune with the current personality of their employees. The question that management must face is, "How can I obtain the best results from the portion of time the individual is devoting to the work quadrant?"

Management Threats

The fear of losing one's job still motivates people. The boss with a whip still exists and produces results, particularly in an environment where jobs are hard to find. But this type of management style requires a great deal of ongoing effort on the part of the manager and does not, in the long run, produce superior performance (see Figures 5.3 and 5.4).

Self-Motivation

This is the best of all worlds. If all employees were self-motivated, management's job would be extremely easy. Figure 5.4 is a picture of how some managers view a self-motivated employee. But in the real world, employees look around and find individuals who are not performing or working as hard as they are and still receiving similar benefits. As a result, in this environment employees tend to be influenced by the poor performers and drop their level of performance down to the level of the poorest performing individual in the group. Self-motivation works with less than 10% of employees.

Management motivation?

FIGURE 5.3
Management motivation.

Self-motivation

FIGURE 5.4
Self-motivation.

Employee Involvement

Employee involvement is, by far, the best way to enhance employees' performance. Involving the individuals in discussions about things that impact their jobs produces improved commitment and increases work ethics. Individuals respond and perform better when they are involved in designing their work process, and understand the reason why something is being done and the value of their efforts.

Once an organization realizes that its success rests in the hands and minds of its employees, and when the employees experience the stimulation and satisfaction of helping the organization improve, participative management will become a way of life and its achievements will continue to grow.

Communicate—Communicate—Communicate

You cannot have too much communication related to a change initiative. Say it once, say it twice, and reinforce it by saying it the third time. Say it when you are talking to an individual and to people in a small group, or large meetings. Resistance goes down as knowledge about the change goes up. For a long time, organizations have been trying desperately to establish effective two-way communications (up and down), and just as we have started to make real progress, we found that this was not adequate. It is management's responsibility to ensure that it covers every new route in the five-way communications (up, down, horizontally, customer, and supplier) as well as communicates an honest, accurate, and realistic picture of the change and its impact upon the organization. We recommend a short 1–2 minute elevator speech be developed and shared by each manager for their personal use. This helps ensure that homogeneous understanding of the change's impact is communicated to the employees.

Town Meetings

Among the most effective communication tools is the town meeting. A town meeting is a relatively loosely structured gathering that anybody interested in the subject can attend. The town meeting usually starts with a very short overview of the subject to be discussed. The meeting is then open to questions and answers. Frequently, individuals are reluctant to ask questions related to a change in a one-on-one situation, but when you put them into a group, they seem to gain confidence and speak up, getting answers to questions that are on their minds. The town meeting basic principle is, "There is no dumb question other than the one that wasn't asked." Other people who attend the meeting often have similar questions but are reluctant or too shy to ask them. Although the town meetings normally are designed to focus on a specific subject, they very often shift to other issues that are bothering management and the employees. Town meetings are an excellent way for management and employees to understand each other and resolve some important issues. I particularly like town meetings when the employees trust in management, and they are not afraid to ask embarrassing questions. Of course, close control should be maintained so the town meeting does not allow discussion about individual behaviors.

The town meeting is not the place to carry on a lengthy debate. When major differences are highlighted, separate meetings are frequently called to discuss and resolve these types of problems.

Usually minutes of the town meeting are prepared and posted on the relevant bulletin boards so that the people who did not attend the meeting learn the key points that were discussed. Normally, the name of the individual asking the question is not included in the minutes.

DEVELOPING THE DESIRE TO CHANGE

Management, more than anyone else, is going to be personally impacted by the transformation to the innovation. Many of their personal traits that were responsible for their success will have to be changed. Whereas the employees are subjected to very positive change experiences as they are empowered to take control of their own destiny, many managers will undergo the reverse experience. Most managers got where they are because they outperformed the other people in the group. Along with the management assignment came the ability to get more things done that they wanted done because suddenly they had many more arms and legs to work with.

In years past, managers felt that they knew what needed to be done (or at least what they thought needed to be done) and told other people to do it. When the job was complete, the manager personally and publicly was credited with getting the job done. Now, suddenly, we are asking management to step back and let the people they outperformed do things their own way, to help these employees develop without ordering them to do things, to give them the credit for ideas that were originally the manager's, and to take the spotlight off themselves and put it on the employee. This is understandably a very difficult adjustment for most managers to make, particularly in a technical environment.

Before we can hope to bring about an attitude adjustment, we must first create a desire to change. This is where innovative change management can be a very effective tool. Management needs to be provided with enough data so they can understand that the pain associated with staying with the present process is greater than the pain they will be subjected to in the new process. To accomplish this, the first part of the training process must be focused on awareness training so that the pain associated with staying with the status quo is thoroughly understood.

Once management understands the pain related to their current situation, they are ready to be introduced to the concepts that will be used to transform the organization from its current state into its future vision. Introducing the management team to these key concepts allows them to understand the pain that they will be subjected to during the change process, and the pain level that will be associated with the future state. This understanding is necessary for the management team as a whole, and each manager as an individual, so that each manager can decide if he or she will embrace the improvement effort, thereby allowing his or her attitude to change. If the balance of pain is not heavier on the status quo side, the desired commitment will not be obtained.

THE NEW MIDDLE MANAGER

Top management is the key to getting an improvement process started, but middle management are the ones who keep it going. If top management truly accepts their role as planners and direction-setters, they become distant to the day-to-day problems that face the business. This puts the middle manager in the role of running the organization and ensuring that it continues to improve. The traditional middle-manager role of "kicking tail and taking names" has to change drastically. The old micromanagement attitude needs to give way to a macromanagement that has a wide viewpoint and understands the interfunctional relationships. The key traits of a new generation middle manager are as follows:

- Develop close working relationships and understanding of their customers.
- Have the capability to focus on the "big picture" and manage it.
- Provide education, guidance, and mentoring to the first-line manager.
- Focus on the process rather than the activities.
- Help employees learn from failure rather than punish them for it.
- Concentrate on why problems occur rather than who caused them.
- Recognize continuous improvement as well as meeting targets.
- Embrace change and act as a change agent.
- Reject requests to make decisions that should have been made at lower levels.
- Place high priorities on networking with other functions.
- Prove a role model for the first-level managers and employees.
- Always be honest and aboveboard.
- Have the ability to sacrifice departmental performance to improve total organizational performance.
- Proactively stimulate upward communication.
- Openly share data with all levels.
- Proactively search out employee ideas and actively support the good ones.

- Always explain why an employee's ideas are rejected.
- Practice consensus decision-making whenever possible.
- Empower the employee who is in contact with the customer to resolve customer problems.
- Encourage first-line managers to empower their employees.
- Communicate priorities and hold to them.
- Establish networks that identify potential negative trends before they become problems.
- Place high priority on prevention of problems.
- Recognize and reward employees who prevent and solve problems.
- Vary the reward process to meet the needs of the awardee and the contribution of the activity to the organization.
- Treat everyone as being equally important.
- Demonstrate the importance of meeting schedules and the urgency of getting the job done without compromising quality.
- Handle more negative situations with a smile than with a frown.
- Place high priority on expanding employee capabilities and responsibilities.
- Always have time to listen to an employee's problem now.
- Help those who request it, if possible.
- Above all, management must be good listeners. They remember that the same letters spell the word "listen" that spell the word "silent."

The importance of the middle manager to the improvement process cannot be overemphasized. Middle managers should provide the parental figure for the first-level managers and the employees. Middle managers are those who shape the management style of the organization's future leaders. They are close enough to the employees that they should be on a first-name basis with all the employees within their organization. They should have knowledge about the individual's performance, strengths, and weaknesses, as well as their career aspirations. As we develop potential future organizational leaders, they frequently move from managing one department to another. But the middle manager is the technology and managerial expert that the new managers, experienced managers, and employees all look up to. In the improvement process, they are the teachers, the coaches, the friends, and the mentors. Whereas top management is the beacon of the improvement process, middle managers are the rudders. They truly make the difference between excellence and mediocrity.

MANAGEMENT'S CHANGE PROCESS

Managers must change before they can expect the employees to change. If management keeps on doing the same old thing, the same old way, they will get the same old results. Improvement must start at the top of the management ladder and flow down layer by layer, washing away the undesirable traits, skills, and behaviors, before it flows on to the next level. We can call this the "waterfall effect." Only after a manager has accepted and embraced the change, can they expect their employees to embrace the change. The change should occur first in top-level management, then in middle-level management, and next, at the first level and supervisor level. The employees should not be expected to change until management has led the way. As the old saying goes, "The employees listen to the tongue in management's mouth, but they follow the tongues in management's shoes." And if both your feet and words do not travel in the same direction, the employees can only assume that management speaks with a forked tongue.

To set the stage for this change, the organization needs to invest in training and preparing the management team for their new roles. Remember, "Training isn't expensive; it's ignorance that is expensive." This training should help the management team progress through the transformation cycle that they will create. This cycle can be compared to reshaping a block of ice. You can chip away at the ice with an ice pick to reshape it. But in this case, you lose a lot of potentially good material. We believe this is the wrong way to go. The correct cycle is to first thaw out the old personality, then reshape it into a more desirable new personality, and freeze the new personality into the daily working habits, practices, and beliefs of the organization. With this approach, about 95% of your management team can be salvaged and progress through the transformation cycle.

INNOVATIVE MANAGER SUMMARY

The role of an organization's management strategy, practices, and behaviors in transforming the organization from an information management system into a freewheeling, highly creative group of dedicated professionals is as important as the technologies developed by the organization. Many organizations are still working on the basic strategy of letting another organization develop the creative/innovative concept. Once the market has accepted their competitor's new product or concept, they move very fast to produce a slightly better, less costly version that is in direct competition with the innovative product the first company came up with. This is the very reason that some organizations do not patent their ideas, because too many of their competition have modified their patents lightly to create a competing product. The first company builds its reputation on being an innovative organization that creates exciting new things, and the second organization builds its reputation on being a continuous improvement organization.

> Many organizations play the game of "follow the leader" like we did when we were children. The problem with that is they are always trying to catch up.
>
> **H. J. Harrington**

Section III

Rewards and Recognition

6

Introduction to Innovative Change Management Tools and Methodologies

THE BASIS FOR CHANGE

When you are not improving, you are standing still, or even worse, you are slipping backward, because your competition is improving. When we do an activity the second time the same way as we did it the first time, it is a sign that we did not learn anything the first time. We need to continuously question everything we do and search for a better way of doing it.

The number of patents per person in Japan far exceeds the similar activities in the United States. In the 1970s, you could get ahead in business just by being better and smarter than Tom Jones across the street and Jerry Smith three blocks over from where you live. Today, you are now competing against them as well as with Dr. Chu in Shanghai, Dr. Shaw in India, and Dr. Bertin in Argentina. In many of these countries, there are fewer government restrictions than in the United States as well as significantly lower wages, which give these parts of the world a significant advantage for mass production items. I am not intimating that our government restrictions are wrong. In many cases, they should be more stringent than they are. I am only pointing out that in other parts of the world there are a number of manufacturing advantages over and above cost of labor. Among them are things like safety controls, water purification, and emission controls.

Yes, the world today with its modern communication systems is your "oyster," but the competition around the world also has the same technology advances available to them. In actual practice, there is very little that is gained from installing the latest information technology, because your competition is installing it, and if you did not install it you would put your organization in a very significant disadvantage. With all of this knowledge base and added brainpower available, new business opportunities are flooding the market. New-product development cycles are being cut in half every 5 years. It is almost as though the world keeps spinning faster and faster and faster. Living standards are much higher than they ever were in the past. Things that used to be "niceties" are now necessities. I can remember when it was a real accomplishment to upgrade from a party telephone line to having your own private line, which required special permission and additional cost.

Who would have ever thought we would come to a point that 5-year-olds would be considered handicapped if they did not have their own telephone and computer. Five years ago, who would have believed that there would be "self-driving" cars on the road? Dr. Ping Koy Lam at the Australian National University has already been successful in teleporting molecules from one location to another and then reformatting these back into their original format. It won't be long before statements like "Beam me up" will be part of our normal vocabulary (see Figure 6.1).

FIGURE 6.1
Beam me up.

The world's first virtual shopping center opened in Korea. All of the products are displayed on LCD screens that allow you to order the items by touching the screen. When you get to the counter, your items are already bagged and ready to go (see Figure 6.2).

We undergo some major transformations in our mother's womb, and these changes within us continue until long after we are buried. Changes in the ways we eat, the amounts of food we have, the amount of work we do, and advances in medical science have greatly extended our life expectancy.

There is no way you can stop it. Outside factors are changing the way we do business and the products we produce, and the market we serve is continuously changing. The successful individual tries to give up his or her old habits for something else that is newer and better. Looking backward, these changes are often not all new and better, but are just new or refinements to what went before them. You have to work hard at staying abreast of the latest innovation concept, or you will find yourself always behind, running as fast as you can to catch up, and always complaining because you don't have what the Joneses have.

FIGURE 6.2
Virtual shopping center.

INTRODUCTION TO REWARDS AND RECOGNITION

A good reward process has eight major objectives, often referred to as "Ingredients of an Organization's Reward Process":

1. To provide recognition to employees who make unusual contributions to the organization to stimulate additional effort for further improvement
2. To show the organization's appreciation for superior performance
3. To ensure maximum benefits from the reward process by an effective communication system that highlights the individuals who were recognized
4. To provide many ways to recognize employees for their efforts and stimulate management creativity in the reward process
5. To ensure that management understands that variation enhances the impact of the reward process
6. To improve morale through the proper use of rewards
7. To reinforce behavioral patterns that management would like to see continued
8. To ensure that the employees recognized are perceived as earning the recognition by their fellow employees

Why does recognition matter? George Blomgren, president of Organizational Psychologists, puts it this way, "Recognition lets people see themselves in a winning identity role. There's a universal need for recognition and most people are starved for it."

7

Rewards and Recognition

REWARD PROCESS HIERARCHY

In this chapter, the word *reward* is defined as something given or offered for a special service or to compensate for effort expended. Rewards can be subdivided into the following categories:

- *Compensation*—to financially reimburse for service(s) provided
- *Award*—to bestow a gift for performance or quality
- *Recognition*—to show appreciation for behaving in a desired way

WHY REWARD PEOPLE?

The most basic behavior is to perform in ways for which we are rewarded. The first lesson we learn is directly related to being rewarded for crying. A baby cries, and he or she is fed or his or her diaper is changed. Later on in life, we learn that if we cry, we get picked up and held. We grow a little older, and we are told to clean our plates and we will get dessert, or to be good, and Santa Claus will bring us a new toy. Later on, we are told that if we clean our rom, we can go to the movies.

Yes, all through our lives, we have been rewarded for acting out a desired behavior, and punished when our behaviors are undesirable as defined by someone else or even by our own self. These rewards make eating the asparagus and mowing the lawn and being good a little more worthwhile. It is important to note that all of these rewards occur relatively close to the time that the desired behavior occurs. If we didn't get the dessert until the following Sunday or go to the movies until next month, or if mother tells us on February 2 that if we are not good, Santa Claus will not bring us a toy, the asparagus would stay on the plate, the clutter would still be on the floor, and we probably would continue misbehaving.

Three factors affect the degree to which the desired behavior is reinforced:

- Type of reward
- Elapsed time between meets or exceeds the performance standard
- The extent to which the behavior meets or exceeds the performance standard

Up to this point, we have discussed direct, tangible, positive stimuli that reward people for acting in a desired behavior mode. There are two other ways to encourage people to behave in a desired manner:

- Negative stimulation
- Humanistic stimulation (recognition)

Negative stimulation takes the form of physical and mental pain within the individuals(s) who does not perform in the desired manner. For example, telling a child who wants to go outside to play that she will have to stay at the table until her plate is clean, or disciplining a child because his room is not picked up, or taking away television rights because a child didn't have his homework done, are all examples of negative stimulation. A manager applies negative mental stimulation to an individual when the manager explains why the person is not performing at an acceptable level. Often, employees will subject themselves to mental pain. We have all walked out of a meeting thinking, "Why did I say that? How dumb can I be?" Really good, conscientious employees will take themselves to task when they do something wrong far more than their managers will.

Although recognition is an intangible reward, its positive impact on behavior is usually very effective and should never be overlooked (e.g., when we put a good report card up on the refrigerator door recognizing that the child has done a good job, or when a teacher displays a particularly good drawing in the classroom).

Definitions

Indirect stimulation: This act normally takes the form of nonfinancial recognition. It benefits the organization by instilling pride and degree of satisfaction in the individual. Typical examples are increasing your office size, giving the new office by a window, trophies or plaques, a new computer, etc.

Direct stimulation: This normally takes the form of financial compensation or activities that are related to financial compensation like salary increases, paid-for trips, paid-for education and/or technical conferences, etc.

Whenever possible, direct and humanistic stimulation should be combined. For example, when someone is promoted, the promotion is indirect stimulation, and the increased salary is direct stimulation. Often, management thinks about rewards and recognition as two separate activities. In truth, recognition is just one element of a total reward structure that is needed to reinforce everyone's desired behavioral patterns. As Don Roux, a Minneapolis-based sales and marketing consultant, states, "They (incentive programs) both motivate people to perform some task or achieve some goal by offering rewards. The desirable performance is rewarded, and rewarded behavior tends to be repeated."

When Xerox won the Malcolm Baldrige Award, the Xerox Business Products and Systems National Quality Award release stated:

Recognition and Rewards: Ensures that Xerox people are encouraged and motivated to practice the new behaviors and use the tools. Both individuals and groups are recognized for their quality improvements – whether that takes the form of a simple thank-you or a cash bonus.

This highlights a very important point. Up to now, we have been talking about rewarding individuals, but that is not enough. In today's environment, the organization needs to encourage teams of people to work together to provide the most efficient, effective, and adaptable organization. If we reward only individuals, we develop an organization of prima donnas who are only interested in doing things that make them look good. It is for this reason that your reward process must include both individual and group rewards.

The complexity of today's environment and the sophistication of today's employees make it necessary to carefully design a reward process that provides the management team with many ways to say "thank you" to each employee, because the things that are valued by one individual may have no impact on another. In addition, the reward process that functioned well in the 1970s is probably inadequate today, because the personalities of most organizations have undergone major changes. The influx of women and various minority groups has had a major impact on the way the reward process needs to be structured.

In today's environment, men's attitudes have changed. The male population is aging, and men are often not the sole breadwinner for the family, causing them to be less financially driven. Because of this, it is easy to see, for example, why time-and-a-half pay is no longer a satisfactory reward for giving up a Saturday for many employees. It is for these reasons that we need to take a fresh look at our reward processes to upgrade them so that they meet the needs of today's organizations and their aggressive goals.

Vince Lombardi said, "Winning isn't everything. It's the only thing." This is true for many people, but for others it is enough to help someone else win. At the Olympics, only one man stands on the top platform to receive the gold medal for cross-country skiing, but without the many people standing along the route to give him water, he would not have won. To these little people (and there are a lot more of us little people than there are gold medal winners), often recognition is simply having someone else acknowledge your worth. Recognition is something everyone wants, needs, and strives to obtain. Studies have shown that people classify recognition as one of the things they value most.

KEY REWARD RULES

The reward process needs to be designed, taking into consideration the following points:

- Organizational culture
- Desired behavioral patterns
- Employee priorities
- Behavior/reward timing relationships
- Ease of use

The reward process must be designed to be compatible with the culture and personality of the organization. Things that may be very desirable in one organization can be quite inappropriate in another.

The reward process should be designed to reinforce existing desired behaviors and new desired behaviors. This means that the desired behaviors need to be defined first. Changes in behavioral patterns are much more difficult to implement than those behavioral patterns that are already part of the organization's culture and only need to be reinforced.

Because of this fact, additional focus needs to be given to the reward process to encourage the employees to commit to the new behavioral patterns.

The employee must perceive the reward as being desirable if it is going to have the desired results. If the employee is a ski buff and is rewarded with tickets to Heavenly Valley Ski Resort, that's definitely a positive reinforcement of a behavioral pattern. If the employee is nearing retirement age, however, the tickets may have no meaning, but increasing his or her retirement benefit can be very motivating. I lecture extensively each year. Being given a plaque as a reward for presenting a paper is more of a bother to me than a reward, but giving me a Cross pen and pencil set fits a functional need that is very important to me and becomes an appreciated reward.

It is important to involve your employees in designing the reward process so that the rewards are meaningful to the employees. In designing your reward process, select a group of representative employees to help design the process. Tell them what your reward budget is, and they will tell you the best way to spend it.

There needs to be a very close relationship in time between when the desired behavior occurred and when the reward is given. To reinforce desired behavior, reward the employee(s) immediately if you can. It is best if you can reward them when they are performing the act. (For example: "I really appreciate you staying late to wait for that customer to come in and get his job. Why don't you take your spouse out to dinner this weekend, and the organization will pay for it?") Too often, managers hold off recognizing desired behavior, hoping that a more meaningful reward can be given later. We advise in these cases to give a small reward right away and a bigger reward later on. With this approach, the employee gets immediate positive reinforcement and an important reminder.

Cut the bureaucracy out of your reward process as much as possible. Give management general guidelines, and eliminate the checks and balances in all but the most significant rewards. For example, an individual should not be given more than three minor awards each year, and no more than 10% of the employees should receive major contribution awards each year. Be sure that the employees are not given special awards for just doing their jobs.

Give the manager the power to give the reward and process the paperwork later. Major rewards should be processed through a Rewards Board to be sure that required standards are met, but there should be a long list of rewards that the manager can give to the employee on the spot (e.g., dinners for two, movie tickets, theater tickets, $50 merchandise certificates, etc.).

TYPES OF REWARDS

Everyone hears "thank you" in different ways. The reward process must take these different needs into account. Some people want money, some want a pat on the back, others want to get exposure to upper management, while still others want to look good in front of their peers. For example, American Express has one awards program that they call, "Great Performer Award Luncheon." Typical activities that won employees invitations to these luncheons were

- One American Express employee bailed a French tourist out of jail in Columbus, Georgia
- Another took food and blankets to travelers stranded at Kennedy Airport

The above are unusual performances for employees to take on their own. However, this is what we need if we want to have empowered employees and a truly world-class organization.

It is easy to see that the reward process is only limited by the creativity of your people and the individuals who design the process. The National Science Foundation study made this point: "The key to having workers who are both satisfied and productive is motivation; that is, arousing and maintaining the will to work effectively – having workers who are productive not because they are coerced, but because they are committed" (Lean TRIZ: How to Dramatically Reduce Product-Development Costs with This Innovative Problem-Solving Tool, CRC Press, 2017, p. 177).

To help structure a reward process, let's divide the rewards into the following categories:

1. Financial compensation
   a. Salary
   b. Commissions
   c. Piecework
   d. Organizational bonuses
   e. Team bonuses
   f. Gainsharing
   g. Goal sharing
   h. Stock options

    i. Stock purchase plans

    j. Benefit programs

2. Monetary awards
   a. Suggestion awards
   b. Patent awards
   c. Contribution awards
   d. Best-in-category awards (e.g., best salesperson, employee of the year, etc.)
   e. Special awards (e.g., president's award)
3. Group/team rewards
4. Public personal recognition
5. Private personal recognition
6. Peer rewards
7. Customer rewards
8. Organizational awards

IMPLEMENTATION OF THE REWARD PROCESS

To develop an effective reward process, many factors have to be taken into consideration. The following guidelines should be considered when developing the reward process for your organization:

- Reward fund—The organization should set aside a specific amount of money that the reward process will use. This amount will set the boundaries that the reward process will operate within.
- Reward task team (RTT)—This team will be used to design or update the reward process.
- Present reward process—The RTT should pull together a list of all of the formal and informal rewards that are used within the organization today.
- Desired behaviors—The RTT should prepare a list of the desired behaviors.
- Present reward process analysis—The present reward process should be reviewed to identify the rewards that are not in keeping with the organization's present and projected future culture and visions.
- Desired behavior analysis—Each desired behavior is now compared to the reward categories to see which category or categories should

be used to reinforce the desired behavior. Each behavior should have at least two ways of rewarding people that practice the behavior.

- Reward usage guide—When the reward process is defined, a reward usage guide should be prepared. This guide should define the purpose of each of the reward categories and the procedures that are used to formally process the reward. This guide will be used to help management and employees to understand the reward process, and to help standardize the way rewards are used throughout the organization.
- Management training—One of the most neglected parts of most management training processes is how to use the reward process. As a result, most managers are far too conservative with their approach to rewards, while others misuse them.

In creating a reward process, consider the following:

- Always have it reinforce desired behaviors.
- Reward for exceptional customer service and performance.
- Publish why rewards are given.
- Create a point system that can be used to recognize teams and individuals for small and large contributions. The employee should be able to accumulate points over time to receive a higher-level reward.
- Structure the reward process so that 50% of the employees will receive at least a first-level reward each year.
- Structure the reward process so that the managers can exercise their creativity and personal knowledge of the recipient in selecting the reward.
- Provide ways that anyone can recognize a person for their contributions.
- Provide an instant reward mechanism.

In a paper by Shelly Sweet (a Palo Alto, California, quality consultant), entitled "Reinforcing Quality," she warns us to avoid the following seven pitfalls:

- Cumbersome procedures are costly to administer.
- Executives or middle managers are not consistently supporting the program.
- Awards are applied inconsistently.
- Unexpected behaviors result.

- Employees perceive that the same employees are rewarded repeatedly.
- Enthusiasm wanes.
- Company cost-cutting curtails the program.

DON'T TURN THE ORGANIZATION UPSIDE DOWN

The participative environment has changed the way many organizations look on the organization chart. In the old-style organization chart, top management was at the top of the pyramid, indicating that everyone below them provided services to top management. The popular notion is that with participative management, the pyramid has been turned upside down, with everyone servicing the employee who, in turn, services the customer. But what could be more unstable than a pyramid resting on its pinnacle? It is obvious that the slightest vibration would cause the upside-down pyramid to topple (see Figure 7.1).

We like to think of the organizational structure more as a square (see Figure 7.2). This way of looking at the organizational structure indicates that all activities are important, that five-way communication exists, and that everyone in the organization has an obligation to make the best use of the organization's resources in their efforts to serve their customers. It also lends itself to the concept that organizations have processes that flow across boundaries to conduct the organization's business. It has the advantage of showing that everyone in the organization has an obligation to service the external customers as well as the internal customers.

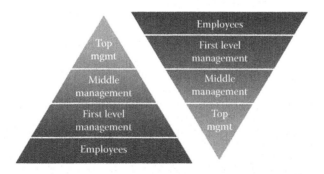

FIGURE 7.1
The organization turned upside down.

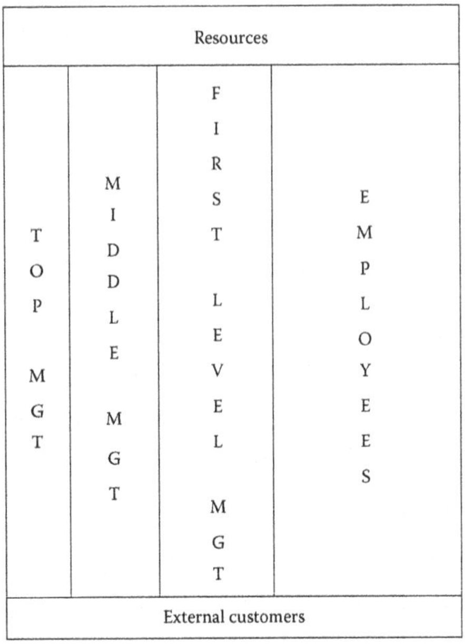

FIGURE 7.2
Preferred organizational model.

REWARD AND RECOGNITION ADVANTAGES AND DISADVANTAGES

Let's look at some of the advantages and disadvantages of the six reward categories.

Advantages of Financial (Money) Rewards

- Its value is understood.
- It is easy to handle.
- The rewardee can select the way it is used.

Disadvantages of Financial (Money) Rewards

- Once it is spent, it is gone.
- If used too often, it can be perceived as part of the employee's basic compensation.
- It is hard to present in a real showmanship manner.
- Often, it is not shared with the family.

Advantages of Merchandise Rewards

- They can appeal to the whole family.
- They have a trophy value.
- They can be used as a progressive reward. (For example, the employee is given points that can be redeemed or accumulated for a higher-level merchandise reward.)
- They cannot be confused with basic compensation.

Disadvantages of Merchandise Rewards

- More administrative time is required.
- A choice of merchandise rewards must be kept in stock.
- There may be other things the rewardee would prefer.

Advantages of Plaques/Trophy Rewards

- Directly tied in to the desired behavior
- Lasts a long time and is never used up
- Customized to the employee (name is often engraved on them)

Disadvantages of Plaques/Trophy Rewards

- May not be valued by the recipient
- Usually not useful
- Often not valued by the family

Advantages of Published Communications

- Can be very specific
- Receive wide distribution
- Inexpensive way of rewarding an individual
- Document is long lasting

Disadvantages of Published Communications

- No tangible value
- Can reduce cooperation and cause envy
- Can be blown out of proportion by the individual in comparison to total contributions over a longer period of time

Advantages of Verbal Communication

- Very personal
- Can be given when the desired behavior occurs
- Least expensive

Disadvantages of Verbal Communication

- Not tangible
- Has no visual reinforcement
- Can be misunderstood

Advantages of Special Privileges
(For example, attend conference, take a business trip, additional vacation days, new equipment, etc.)

- Recipient can be involved in the selection
- Can meet unique employee needs
- Highly valued by employees
- Can be used to support organizational objectives

Disadvantages of Special Privileges

- Can cause envy
- Can impact the organization's operation when the individual is not available
- Can be expensive

To be the most effective, the reward process should combine different reward media, thereby taking advantage of the positive impacts that each have and offsetting their disadvantages. For example, an individual incident could be reinforced by presenting the recipient with a check and a plaque at a department meeting.

Good behavior = Rewards and recognition = Better behavior

Basically, the following media are used individually or in combination to produce desired behavior:

1. Money
2. Merchandise

3. Plaques/trophies
4. Published communications
5. Verbal communication
6. Special privileges

A well-designed reward process will use all six, because each has its own advantages and disadvantages. One of the biggest mistakes management makes is to use the same motivating factors for all employees. People are moved by different things because we all want different things. The reward process needs to be designed to meet the following basic classifications of needs:

- Money
- Status (ego)
- Security
- Respect

PEOPLE WANT RECOGNITION

After the organization has provided the employee with a paycheck and health coverage, what more can or should the organization do for the employee? Management is obligated to do more than just eliminate their financial worries. Employees excel when they are happy, satisfied, and feel that someone else appreciates the efforts they are putting forth. A tangible and intangible reward process can go a long way to fulfilling these needs when properly used.

Research has proven that when management rewards employees for adopting desired behaviors, they work harder and provide better customer service. The benchmark service organizations are more likely to have well-defined and well-used approaches for telling their employees that they are important individuals. Individuals in the world-class organizations that go beyond expectations are held up as customer heroes and role models for the rest of the organization. This provides a continually more aggressive customer performance standard for the total organization.

8

Project Change Management and Culture Change Management Tools and Methodologies

INTRODUCTION

Table 8.1 is a list of the Emergent innovative change management (ICM) tools. These are tools and exercises that are designed to aid the interviewed individual or team in solving problems and be more creative related to their work assignment. They are also designed to stimulate sleeping brain cells so that they are more creative.

I will admit that the list in Table 8.1 is a little overwhelming. But do not worry about being able to use all of these. I don't know anyone who is using the total list of tools in their ICM activities. I personally use approximately 25 of the tools listed when working with clients. The typical change agent within an organization can get by knowing only 15 of the tools. Of course, the more ICM tools that your change agent is familiar with, the better he or she can customize an ICM project to meet the specific needs of the organization's specific project.

There is a list of mind-expanding tools and exercises that are designed to stimulate sleeping brain cells so that they are more creative in Appendix C. The brain is a muscle and needs to be exercised on a regular schedule very much like you exercise the other muscles in your body. These mind expanders are designed to provide you with an exercise program for your mind designed to make you more creative and innovative.

TABLE 8.1

Change Management Toolkit

- 4S Realignment
- 7S Analysis
- Action Plan
- Align Systems and Structures: Phase Diagnostic
- Behavior Targeting
- Case for Change
- Change Assessment
- Change Impact Mapping
- Change Leader Assessment
- Change Management Overview Presentation
- Communication Action Plan
- Communication Strategy
- Communications Campaign Planner
- Control-Influence Analysis
- Create Urgency: Phase Diagnostic
- Current-Future State Analysis
- Elevator Pitch
- Engage the Stakeholders: Phase Diagnostic
- Event Planning Template
- Executive Sponsorship Assessment
- Focus Group Process
- Force Field Analysis
- In Frame/Out of Frame
- Influencing Strategies
- Is/Is Not
- Keeping Up the Pressure
- Key Stakeholders Map
- Lead the Change: Phase Diagnostic
- Manager Enrollment Plan
- Measurement Audit
- Measurement-Reward Cycle
- Need-Vulnerability Assessment
- Past Experience Profile
- Phases of Transition Model
- Plan the Change: Phase Diagnostic
- Progress Review
- Project-Change Leadership Matrix
- RACI
- Resistance Profiler
- Reverse Imaging
- Scoping Questions
- Self-Assessment of Personal Change Agility
- SIPOC

(*Continued*)

TABLE 8.1 (*Continued*)

Change Management Toolkit

- Stakeholder Adoption Map
- Stakeholder Analysis
- Stakeholder Interview Process
- Stakeholder Position Map
- Stakeholder Prioritization Matrix
- Stakeholder Role Analysis
- Stakeholder-Specific Communication Action Plan
- Sustain the Change: Phase Diagnostic
- System-Structure Impact Analysis
- Team Capability Assessment
- Team Charter
- Team Effectiveness Assessment
- Team Operating Agreement
- Teamwork Model
- Threat-Opportunity Matrix
- Tracking Progress Checklist
- Visioning Process
- Wordstorming

DIFFERENT APPROACHES TO ICM

Different organizations have restructured and organized these tools and their activities in unique ways to create their own special methodologies. The following is a list of 12 organizations that specialize in the ICM methodology along with the name of the methodology the individual organizations use. Do not be fooled—just because the change in their methodology is different does not mean that the content within the methodology is different.

1. The Universal Change Activation Toolkit
2. ADKAR Model for Change Management
3. AIM (Accelerating Implementation Methodology)
4. Beckhard and Harris Change Management Process
5. Boston Consulting Group (BCG) Change Delta
6. Bridges Leading Transition Model for Change
7. Harrington Voehl Sustainable Change Model
8. GE's Change Acceleration Process (CAP)
9. John Kotter Eight Step Model for Change

10. McKinsey 7S Change Model
11. Kurt Lewin's Three Stage Change Model
12. People Centered Implementation (PCI) Mode

FIVE TYPES OF CHANGE ASSESSMENT

We suggest using five types of change assessments to measure performance level:

1. Innovation Maturity Analysis
2. Change History Analysis
3. Employee Opinion Survey
4. Customer Focus Groups
5. Is/Should Be Analysis

Assessment 1: Innovation Maturity Analysis

This is an analysis of the five Major Innovation Areas in a typical organization:

A. Management
B. Product
C. Processes
D. Sales and marketing
E. Support

For each of these five Major Innovation Areas, enough items need to be evaluated so that a minimum of 7 of the 10 Innovation Drivers (10S) are used to measure the performance level (see Table 8.2).

Management is responsible for determining how the resources within the organization will be utilized. Getting a proper picture of the AS/IS situation is absolutely critical to make meaningful decisions. Management should be sure that the information it is using to make a decision reflects the reality as seen by the executive team, Board of Directors, middle management, line management, employees, and current and potential customers. It must be sure that the assessment covers the proper considerations and that the data that the assessment team present are accurate as reported.

TABLE 8.2

Ten Innovation Drivers (10S)

1. Shared Vision
2. Strategy
3. Systems
4. Structure
5. Skills
6. Styles/Personality
7. Staffing
8. Systematic Change Management
9. Specialized Technology/Information Technology Systems
10. Situated Knowledge Management

Assessment 2: Change History Analysis

This assessment analyzes 14 different factors to identify the present enablers related to innovation within the organization. This allows us to focus on improving the use of each of the enabling factors to bring about major improvement within the organization in a minimum amount of time as they are already in line with the present organization's culture. It will also identify those factors that are having a negative impact upon innovation at the present time so that plans can be put in place to minimize the impact and to convert them to enabling factors. Change history analysis measures the degree of support or resistance an organization will encounter based on an individual's impression of previous projects he or she has been involved in.

Basically, this analysis is used to understand the impact that past change experience had on the individual's attitudes and beliefs. The following is a list of 14 factors that have either a positive or negative impact on the project's results. The individual taking the survey will rate each of the 14 factors on a 10-point scale with a *rating of 1* indicating strong disagreement with the statement and a *rating of 10* indicating strong agreement with the statement:

1. Amount—The number of alterations required by the change.
2. Scope—The range or span of the organization affected by the change.
3. Time—The amount of time people have to implement the change.
4. Transferability—The degree to which the change is easy to communicate and will be understood.
5. Predictability—The degree to which people can accurately anticipate the effect of the change on them.

6. Ability—The degree to which people feel they have or can attain the knowledge and skills necessary to implement the change.
7. Willingness—The degree to which people are motivated to implement the change.
8. Values—The degree to which people must change some of their strongly held beliefs about the way they are operating.
9. Emotions—The extent to which the change requires people to feel differently about other people or operating procedures.
10. Knowledge—The degree to which the change requires people to learn new information or view existing information differently than they have in the past.
11. Behaviors—The extent to which the change requires people to modify their daily routine of job-related activities.
12. Logistics—The degree to which the change requires any significant alteration in employee job procedures, such as scheduling, time management, and equipment utilization.
13. Economics—The degree to which the change requires people to operate differently regarding budgets, expenses, or funding.
14. Politics—The degree to which people must modify their current methods of influencing others, utilizing power, working in a team, dealing with territoriality, and protecting vested interests

There are three category performance levels:

- Category I: Low Risk—Enabler (average score of 1, 2, or 3)
  The change management plan should be aimed at getting all of the parameters operating at this effective level.
- Category II: Caution Range (average score of 4, 5, or 6)
  Parameters classified at these levels have a moderate risk of causing a disruption to the projects. The culture change management (CCM) team should be targeting to get 80% of parameters classified in this range or the enabler range after the first 24 months of the CCM project.
- Category III: High Risk—Barrier (average score of 7, 8, 9, or 10)
  Any item in this range indicates a high level of disruption causing the individual changes to fail or to be less effective than they should be. Early priority should be placed on improving the parameters that fall into this range.

Assessment 3: Employee Opinion Survey

An employee opinion survey is primarily directed at defining the status of morale and each member of the organization's commitment to the organization. It is used to evaluate immediate managers' and higher-level managers' as well as each employee's level of satisfaction with the organization and the jobs he or she is assigned to.

It is useful to conduct employee opinion surveys, which are usually made up of 60–80 questions, every 18–24 months. We like to analyze the data as they relate to each natural work team. Often, the negative impact on innovation occurs even at lower levels than the major innovation areas. Different natural work teams have different problems based on the personality of the individual who is managing and networking. This allows you to identify individual managers who need special attention in order to increase innovation and creativity within the organization. This often happens when a very strong technical person is managing the natural work team and uses its members primarily as a means for him or her to get more of his or her ideas evaluated and implemented (i.e., one brain with many arms). Typical questions that might be asked are as follows:

1. Is your manager open to your suggestions?
2. Are you being paid fairly compared to what you would be earning in a similar organization?
3. How supportive is the second-level manager to give you a fair hearing?
4. Are you being treated fairly related to promotional opportunities?

In analyzing employee opinion surveys, the average for each natural work team for each question should be compared to the organization's total average for that question. Questions with ratings that are statistically positive or negative should be highlighted in the report. It is absolutely essential that the natural work team assessment results be reported back to the members of the natural work team. They are the very best ones to make recommendations on how to improve them in the future.

Assessment 4: Customer Focus Groups

Customer focus groups provide first-hand data on how internal or external customers would like the organization to change. These group meetings with the external customers allow the focus group leader to probe deeply into the areas where the external customers feel there is opportunity for improvement and a new product. They also allow external customers to express their feelings as part of the group. Although customer focus groups are an assessment tool that is primarily used with external customers, we find it is even more effective at identifying potential weaknesses within the organization. It provides a view by the members of the organization that we frequently get in a group environment that we do not get on individual feedback.

The facilitator of a focus group should always have a list of probing questions to present to the participants. The facilitator should lead the conversation in the direction that the participants are interested in discussing.

For new product focus groups with external customers and potential customers, it is often advantageous to start the meeting by presenting the organization's view of all of the technology that will progress over the next 5–10 years.

Basically, there are three types of external customer focus groups:

- Getting the external customers' view related to new product that will go on sale at a specific time. (Would you buy this?).
- Getting the external customer's view on product that is being developed with no specific time set for the product to go on sale. It is designed to answer the question, "What features should this product have, and what is the maximum price they would pay for the product?" It is primarily focused on what value the external customer places on specific potential products. It is usually used in conjunction with the value proposition or business case approval.
- Getting the external customer's view on what new product and services are to be developed. It is primarily used to get input into research and development to direct their research activities.

Assessment 5: Is/Should Be Analysis

The is/should be analysis is a series of questions that are each evaluated in three different ways:

1. How is it today?
2. What should it be 3 years from now?
3. What level priority does the transformation have?

These three points of view provide a means to time an individual question based on how important it is that a specific change occurs. Based on these five data inputs, one or more reports are generated that define the strengths and weaknesses in the organization's approach to innovation, creativity, and change management. These reports serve as the foundation for the change management plans that are developed in Activity 3.

This is a tool that is frequently used in setup and prioritizes innovation improvement opportunities. It is particularly effective because it considers today's performance, where you would like to see performance take place in the future, and the priority that the change has in the project plan. It also is an effective tool at identifying inhibitors and priorities at the various levels within the organization. We frequently find that the executive's viewpoint of organizational problems is not an accurate observation, because the executive is viewing the system looking down on rather than looking up and using. A good example of this is the healthcare package given to members of Congress in comparison to the healthcare package provided by the Affordable Care Act.

Assessment Report

Does every organization need to use all five of these assessment tools in order to improve their culture? Personal experience indicates that in many cases the executive team is so anxious for the organization to become more innovative that they are unwilling to spend a sufficient amount of time to understand the situation. The assessment and planning part of the innovation cultural change is the least expensive and can have the biggest positive impact on the outcome from the cultural change.

One word of warning: Do not treat the feedback reports as criticizing the way you manage your organization. Seldom do managers get the opportunity to understand what their employees are really thinking. In most U.S. companies, it is the "yes" men or women who get the promotions and big money. It is absolutely true that most managers like the following statement better than any other statement, "Wow, Boss! That is a fantastic idea. I wish I had come up with it. What do you want me to do to implement it?" What they don't want to hear is, "Boss, your idea will not work. We have to do it this way." In actuality, the second statement is the statement that your management team needs to accept and welcome as the organization changes to a more innovative/creative culture.

I remember one assessment feedback session I had with the president of a large organization (650 employees) and the rest of the executive committee. He was personally enraged that any of his employees would make these ratings. He first accused me of falsifying the data to make him look bad and get the consultant job. He then turned to the executive committee and stated, "Stand up if you rated any of these three or lower. I want to know who the uninformed managers are." He later explained, "My employees think I am great. No one starts work before I do. I know that because I have the only key that will let people in. When the start work bell rings, I personally do a walk through the total area so I will know who is out ill and see that someone backs up his or her job." (As a side note, needless to say I didn't get the contract to help them implement total quality management and prepare their operating manual.)

PERFORMANCE IMPROVEMENT MANAGEMENT

The ICM methodology is most often used in conjunction with problem solving or taking advantage of an opportunity. (New product development and production fall under the category of taking advantage of an opportunity.) The change process that supports problem-solving and taking advantage of opportunities is divided into three phases:

- Phase I—Defining how the organization needs to change
- Phase II—Defining what the organization needs to change
- Phase III—Managing the organization's change process

Figure 8.1 identifies the phases and activities in the performance improvement management methodology.

- Phase I—Defining How the Organization Needs to Change: Developing Future-State Visions.
    - Activity I.1. Conduct a present-state assessment.
    - Activity I.2. Develop key business drivers' vision statements.
    - Activity I.3. Develop improvement performance goals.
    - Activity I.4. Define desired behaviors and habit patterns.
- Phase II—Defining What the Organization Needs to Do to Change.
    - Activity II.5. Develop the individual performance improvement management plans.

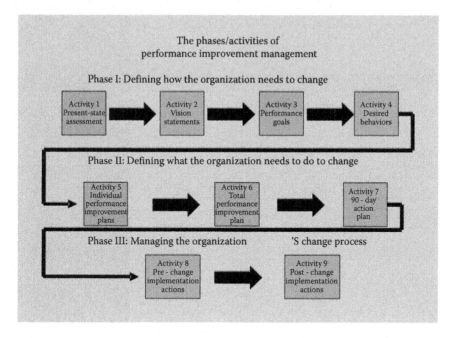

FIGURE 8.1
Three phases of performance improvement management methodology.

- Activity II.6. Combine the individual performance improvement management plans (total performance improvement management plan).
- Activity II.7. Develop a 90-day action plan.
- Phase III—Managing the Organization's Change Process.
  - Activity III.8. Execute prechange implementation actions.
  - Activity III.9. Execute postchange implementation actions.

It must be considered that there is nothing more difficult to carry out, nor more doubtful of success, nor more dangerous to handle, than to initiate a new order of things.

Prince Machiavelli
Sixteenth-Century Italian Statesman

9

Suggestion Programs

Up to this point, we have been talking about suggestions and ideas that are within the employee's job description. Now we want to discuss ideas that are outside of the employee's responsibility, for example, a secretary who suggests use of a different printer because it would improve productivity; a test operator who suggests redesigning a test fixture so the parts cannot be put in backward; or the repair technician who suggests using a different part because it will last longer in a specific application. These are all good ideas that will save the organization money and improve its reputation. As a result, the organization should be willing to share the savings from these ideas with the employees who made the suggestions. Usually, the scope of the suggestions requires that someone other than the suggester implements the suggestions or at least approves the suggestions before they can be implemented. As a result, these suggestions are submitted into a formal suggestion program.

All individuals and all ideas are eligible for the improvement effectiveness program. Many suggestions are not eligible for the suggestion program. The best approach is to evaluate an idea to see if it is eligible for the suggestion program, and if it is not then turn it in under the improvement effectiveness program after it has been implemented. The key elements of the suggestion program are as follows:

1. The suggestion must not be part of the suggester's responsibility.
2. The suggestion does not have to be implemented to be considered.
3. The suggester shares in the savings resulting from the suggestion.
4. The suggestion cannot be pre-dated by activities or plans already under way.

How does the suggestion process work? National Cash Register Company developed the concept back in 1896. The value of the suggestion program is that it offers the person closest to the work activity the opportunity to suggest improvements. This results in more effective utilization of assets, increased productivity, waste reduction, lower product costs, and improved quality. As Paul Peterman, then manager of the Field Suggestions at IBM Corporation, put it, "Ideas are the lifeblood of the company, and the suggestions plan is a way of getting these ideas marketed."

The formal suggestion process requires that employees document their ideas for improvement and submit them to a central suggestion department that is responsible for coordinating and evaluating the ideas and reporting back to the employee. The suggestion department reviews each suggestion and chooses an area within the organization that is best suited to evaluate the suggestion. The evaluation area studies the recommended changes to determine if they will provide overall improvement in quality, cost, or productivity. If the suggestion is accepted by the evaluation area, the evaluator will determine what tangible savings will result from implementing the idea.

In some cases, suggestions will be adopted even though the savings are intangible. These ideas benefit the organization, but the savings cannot be measured or estimated in a precise dollar amount. If the idea is rejected, the investigator records the reason why the idea was rejected on the evaluation form. Both the accepted and rejected suggestions are then returned to the suggestion department, where the evaluations are reviewed for completeness and accuracy. A letter is then sent to the employee's manager describing the action that was taken on the suggestion. For an accepted suggestion, a check normally accompanies the letter. Each suggestion is then reviewed with the employee by the employee's manager. When major cash awards are received, the manager will usually call a department meeting to present the award to the employee, to publicly recognize the employee as well as to provide an incentive to get the other members of the department participating in the suggestion program.

Paul Revere Insurance Company employees submitted 20,000 suggestions during the first three years of their improvement process. The suggestions were a major contributor to the organization's improved performance:

- Income up 200% with no additional staff
- Organization moved from number 2 to number 1 in their field of insurance

Frank K. Sonnenberg, in his article entitled, "It's a Great Idea...But," wrote, "A new idea, like a human being, has a life cycle. It is born. If properly nurtured, it grows. When it matures, it becomes a productive member of society." He points out that at 3M, some people claim that the company's "11th commandment" is, "Thou shalt not kill an idea" (https://www.questia.com/magazine/1G1-12112236/it-s-a-great-idea-but).

PROBLEMS WITH U.S. SUGGESTION PROGRAMS

The major reasons that suggestion programs are not as effective as they should be in the United States are as follows:

- Lack of management involvement
- Long evaluation cycles
- Lack of goal setting
- Lack of recognition

Too often, management uses the suggestion program as a way of putting off the employee. Instead of listening to the employee's ideas, they say, "Write it up and turn it in as a suggestion." The manager's job in the idea generation process is to

- Encourage employees to express their ideas
- Help them clarify their thoughts
- Determine if the idea is eligible for the suggestion program or if it should be used in the performance improvement program
- Support good ideas to help them get implemented quickly

We have found that the quantity of employee suggestions is directly proportional to the manager's interest in the suggestions process. Each department should set a target for the number of suggestions that the department will submit every 3 months. This helps make the suggestion program a challenge for the department and its members.

GETTING IDEAS FLOWING

For the average organization, it is easy to embrace the concept of tapping the hidden powers of the employees' ideas. The problem is, how do you do it? How do you keep your credibility with the employees if they start turning in ideas and swamp the process? A good way to tap into this reservoir of ideas and not open the floodgates is to hold an "idea week." In this approach, management announces to the employees that a specific week will be set aside to see how many improvement ideas can be generated. For example, "The week of January 16–21 will be set aside to see how many ideas can be turned in that will improve safety and quality or reduce costs."

This is an excellent approach to getting the idea process flowing. It allows the organization to develop the idea processing system under a controlled environment. It will also help to define any problems that need to be corrected before the formal process is implemented. Many organizations will repeat this cycle two or three times before introducing the formal ongoing suggestion process.

IDEA SHARING

An important part of developing a creative environment within an organization is the open sharing of the ideas that are generated. Many organizations accomplish this by maintaining a list of new and creative ideas that is made available to the entire organization. Often these data are stored in a computer database that can be sorted in many different ways, providing a valuable database to help solve future problems.

3M Corporation has made use of "Innovation Fairs" to exhibit new ideas. Employees from product engineering, marketing, production, and other departments attend these fairs to gain new ideas and to discuss the ideas that are being exhibited with their creators.

PROBLEMS WITHOUT KNOWN SOLUTIONS

No matter how good an organization is or how well employees are trained, there will always be a few problems that cannot be solved by the person who recognized them and questions that the employees would like to get answers for. In these cases, the first approach that an employee should try is to talk with his or her manager. Often, an employee's level of trust is low, and the employee may believe that his or her manager will just put them off.

Other employees are just too meek to discuss the situation with their manager because they feel that they will bother him or her with little things or things that they should already know the answer to. To offset this situation, we need to provide all employees with other ways to get their problems solved and their questions answered.

REQUEST FOR CORRECTIVE ACTION

Most managers think that they know all the problems that are plaguing the organization. We have seen managers who have told their employees, "Don't bring problems to me without your suggested solutions. I already know what the problems are. What I need is help in solving them." The real truth of the matter is that most managers do not know about most of the problems that are preventing their employees from doing an excellent job. In a study designed by Sidney Yoshida, a leading Japanese consultant, he reported that

- 4% of the organization's problems were known by top management
- 9% of the organization's problems were known by middle management
- 74% of the organization's problems were known by supervisors
- 100% of the organization's problems were known by the employees

Of course, we all know that priorities are set by this same top management who knows about only 4% of the total problems. The use of a request for corrective action (RCA) process provides a way for the employee to inform management about the problems that the present process shields them from. The RCA process is a very effective way of identifying the submerged problems before they tear the bottom out of the organization's ship. Any employee who is having a problem or knows of a problem can fill out an RCA form and send it in to the improvement control center. The writer has the option of signing or not signing the RCA, with the stipulation that he or she will remain anonymous, unless the employee designates a desire to discuss the situation with the investigator.

Organizations that have implemented this type of program indicate that over 90% of the items submitted can be acted on and brought to a successful conclusion.

SPEAK-UP PROGRAM

Another way to relieve pent-up emotion and provide the employee with answers to the questions is through a "speak-up program." This program encourages employees to share with the organization the problems they are having or questions that they may have about the organization and its activities so the situation can be corrected or explained. The speak-up program is confidential and never divulges the employee's name. It provides an ombudsman to represent the employee without writing the employee's name. These speak-up programs allow employees to point out inadequacies in the way they are being managed to bring about positive change within the organization.

HOW TO GET CREATIVITY, INNOVATION, INVOLVEMENT, AND PARTICIPATIVE MANAGEMENT TO THRIVE

The following is a list of requirements for employee innovation, involvement, and participative management to thrive within the work environment:

- Management will have to share the power and responsibility.
- Management must provide the employees with much more information than they have in the past.
- Participative management/employee involvement needs to be practiced at all levels of management.
- Management needs to trust their employees in order to earn the trust of all the employees.
- Management needs to feel comfortable with decentralized decision-making.
- Management needs to stop performing hindsight appraisals.
- Management must encourage an environment where failures are accepted as being part of the learning cycle, and risk-taking is a dominant trait of the people who get ahead.
- Time must be made available to train the employees in how to make decisions, learn new jobs, and perform business analysis.
- Management must have the courage to reject a poor solution but take time to explain why the suggestion is being rejected.

Section IV

Project Change Management (PCM)

10

Project Change Management
Introduction

OVERVIEW OF PROJECT CHANGE
MANAGEMENT METHODOLOGY

Project change management (PCM) is a part of project management activities. (Note: We are using the term project change management for this methodology, although the methodology can be used in activities other than project activities. For example, it could be used in acquisitions, legal, process improvement, personnel replacement, improvement activities, program activities, portfolio maintenance, organizational alignment, etc. Throughout this book the word program reflects all of these different personnel-related activities.) PCM is directed at the people side of a project; it helps prepare the people who could have their work lives changed as a result of the project to become committed to the change. PCM often prepares the employees so well that they look forward to the change. (Note: This is not part of "A Guide to the Project Management Body of Knowledge" [PMBOK] concept.) The PCM part of project management activities consists of

- PCM planning: Define the level of resistance to change, and prepare a plan to offset the resistance.
- Define roles and develop competencies: Identify who will serve as sponsors, change agents, change targets, and change advocates and then train each individual on how to perform the specific role.
- Establish burning platform: Define a situation where the major cost of the status quo becomes prohibitively expensive. In such circumstances, major change is not just a good idea—it is a business imperative. This is discussed later in this chapter.

- Transformation management: Implement the PCM plan. Test for gaps in management support (black holes), lack of acceptance of the transformation activities, and loss of commitment to the project.

Another support pattern that helps explain change is the various roles that must be played to support implementation of the PCM methodology.

PCM METHODOLOGY ROLES, AUTHORITY, AND RESPONSIBILITIES

There are a number of project-specific "jobs" (e.g., project manager) necessarily created as another dimension by adding PCM to a project plan. These roles are split into four general categories as described in the following text. The larger projects should have at least one individual assigned as a project team member who has had detailed training in PCM. For smaller projects, the PCM methodology can be divided between members of the project management team. This requires individual training for those individuals assigned to spend part-time duties as a part of the ICM process. Before we go any further, we need to define the individual roles people play in the formal PCM methodology.

Change Facilitator

The change facilitator plays a critical role in ICM activities. Because of this, we take a little more time explaining the assignment and the personnel requirements for this assignment. The change facilitator is the individual who leads and directs the ICM activities for a project. He or she provides the just-in-time PCM training and ICM guidance to the improvement team, sponsors, and others requiring some ICM training. The change facilitator can be viewed as a "Black Belt." Change agents are often internal or external consultants who serve as the change facilitators.

At some point during most projects, the project manager will be required to perform each of these roles:

- Change agent
- Change facilitator
- Sustaining sponsor

The change facilitator must have the training and experience to under-stand PCM concepts and apply them to the specific project. He or she will serve as the PCM authority and trainer for the project. The change facilita-tor assesses the organization's resistance level to the project and prepares the PCM plan and its integration into the overall project plan. Once the plan is prepared, the change facilitator will be held responsible for imple-mentation of the plan.

The change facilitator should be one of the first members of the project team to be identified, as he or she will play an important role in help-ing the project manager select project team members who can embrace key change concepts. The people who make up a project are a key PCM consideration. In small projects, the change facilitator assignment can be handled by the project manager if he or she has the proper level of training, but for major projects, an individual should be assigned who has PCM as a sole responsibility. Not everyone can be the change facilitator. Too often, organizations feel that because an individual has attended a PCM class or read a book on PCM, that the individual is capable of performing the role of the change facilitator. Of course, this is not true. If you catego-rize people as being one of the following four types, the change facilitator would need to be effective in all four but must be extremely good in the sensor (networker) role:

- Planners
- Doers
- Leaders
- Networkers
- Networkers learned

Only people who feel very comfortable functioning in sensor roles and who are already experienced networkers should be considered for the change facilitator. The change facilitator needs to have and maintain a network of contacts that serve as sensors that define the level of organi-zational resistance. The facilitator needs to be able to identify potential "black holes" before they become a bottleneck in the project. He or she must be skilled in using problem-solving techniques and team skills. In addition, the change facilitator should be experienced in adult education concepts. The change facilitator should also understand the organization's big picture and have knowledge of any other projects that are going on or will be started that relate to the same group of people who will be affected by this project. But most of all, the change facilitators must have excellent people skills and be very knowledgeable about how people react to different conditions.

The change facilitators and the change agents have a lot of common skills. Usually there will be only one change facilitator assigned to a project. This facilitator will provide training to the inexperienced change agents who are assigned to the project. Often, highly skilled technical people need to serve part-time as change agents as well as implementing their specific technical change into the new process. Because the change facilitator must have an in-depth understanding of the change process and have extensive past experience in effectively using the change methodologies, outside consultants are often used for this job. In large organizations that are undergoing a lot of change, special individuals who have effectively functioned as change agents on a number of projects are often designated as change facilitators. In cases where the change agents assigned to the project already have the skills to do their assigned tasks and can provide the required PCM training to the project team, advocates, targets, and sponsors, a change facilitator need not be assigned to the project team.

Black Hole

Definition

Black hole is a condition where one or more manager fails to fulfill his/her sponsor responsibilities, such as by withholding or distorting information so that it doesn't get distributed to the rest of the organization.

The expression "black holes" is borrowed from the field of astrophysics, in which it applies to those areas in space that have a gravitational pull so strong that everything—including light—is drawn in. There are spots in the corporate universe that exert the same effect. It is common for management bureaucracy structures to allow these to vanish without a trace. Like a black hole in space that captures everything that travels in its vicinity, various levels of management withhold or distort information so that it does not pass on to the rest of the organization. Without proper information, change will fail.

Take, for example, a recent reengineering project that was announced to an organization. The initiating sponsor of the project was the president, who personally gave a presentation to the extended management team enlisting their support. Furthermore, the project team made numerous status updates to the steering committee at open forms. However, there were still complaints and misunderstandings surrounding the level of commitment needed for the project. It was discovered that the majority of the managers believed that with the personal involvement of the president and ongoing communications from the project team, little was required on their part. This became a "black hole." Finally, in order to achieve the results expected by the project, the initiating sponsor established an expectation of the sponsors and reinforced them with the appropriate consequences. It is important to realize that with all the downsizing, rightsizing, restructuring, reengineering, redesign, and planning of the organization and self-managed work teams, middle and first-line managers have suffered a percentage of reduction more than double that of the nonmanagerial workforce.

Sponsor

A sponsor is the individual or group who has the power to sanction or legitimize the activity. Sponsors create an environment that enables the changes caused by the project to be made on time and within budget. There are two types of sponsors: initiating and sustaining. An initiating sponsor is the person (or group) who has the power and resources to actually start the change process. Sustaining sponsors use their logistics, their economic and political proximity, to assist the targets (i.e., the people who actually have to change the way they work) to ensure that the initiating sponsor's directives are implemented.

Definition

The **initiating sponsor** is the person or group with the power and resources to start the change process.

The **sustaining sponsors** use their logistics, the economic and/or political proximity to assist the targets (the individual or group affected by the change), to ensure that the initiating sponsor's directions are implemented.

Advocates

An advocate is the individual or group who wants to achieve a change but lacks the power to sanction it. The job of the advocates is to persuade potential initiating and sustaining sponsors to support the project and to keep the sponsors' interest up to the level that is necessary to make the project successful.

Too often, a sponsor, who was initially sold on a project, loses interest or lacks the time to pursue it at the necessary level. When this occurs, he or she becomes dysfunctional as a sponsor. The advocate, who is assigned to each sponsor, is responsible for recognizing when this occurs and needs to take appropriate action to revitalize the sponsor. The advocate supports the project and is responsible for keeping the sponsor's interest up to the level that is necessary to make the project successful.

> Change ideas can die an early death if those who conceived them do not communicate them to the people who can make it happen.
>
> **H. J. Harrington**

Change Agent

A change agent is the individual or group responsible for facilitating the implementation of the change. The success of the agent depends on his or her ability to diagnose potential problems, develop a plan to deal with these problems, and manage human issues of the change process effectively. These are individuals or groups who are responsible for actually making the change. A change agent's success depends on the ability to diagnose potential problems and develop a plan to deal with these issues of the change process effectively.

Professional Staff

The professional staff are the individuals who prepare the work breakdown structures and budgets and who perform the actual work required to implement the change (e.g., engineers, programmers, and industrial engineers).

Target (Sometimes Called "Impacted Employee")

The target is the individual or group affected by the change. Targets must be educated to understand the changes they are expected to accommodate, and they must be involved appropriately in the implementation process. These are the individuals or groups affected by the change. Targets must be educated to understand the changes they are expected to accommodate, and they must be involved appropriately in the implementation process.

FIGURE 10.1
Wearing a different hat.

Role assignments for change projects follow a linear path through an organization. Working relationships can be highly complex and convoluted, with people often playing more than one role and frequently shifting roles once the change is underway. The professional staff must be skilled change agents who allow them to switch hats from the technical work to the change agent activities many times during the project (see Figure 10.1).

THREE BASIC ORGANIZATIONAL STRUCTURES

We have found that as much as 80% of the time organizations are not reaping the rewards they should from the triangular relationships made up of the sponsor, the change agent, and the targets. This poor track record stems from sponsors attempting to delegate to their agents the power to authorize the change. That works fine when sponsors assign an agent the responsibility of actually rolling up their sleeves and putting the change into effect. However, sponsors cannot pass on sanctioning power to people who do not hold that status with the targets (see Figure 10.2).

Having agents tell targets who do not report to them what to do almost always fails. Such attempts to influence may work for minor changes but rarely work in major transitions. The inappropriate attempts by support staff to pressure line managers into complying with their wishes is at the heart of much of the line-versus-staff conflict so prevalent in today's organizations. The true culprit in such situations is usually not the support staff, but the sponsors. Sponsors turn to their human resources director

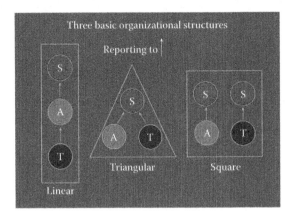

FIGURE 10.2
Three basic organizational structures.

and say, "Go tell the line that they must use the new hiring procedure; that's what I pay you for." Or they say to the head of information services, "Force them to use the new system if you have to. That's your job." In effect, the mandate is, "Tell people who don't report to you what they must do." Of course, when this message meets a brick wall, it is the agent who takes the heat for not doing his or her job.

Triangular configurations, however, are not the true source of the problem. Triangles are a natural formation in any organization. The problem lies in too few people understanding the dynamics that govern triangular relationships. You cannot manage such relationships if you do not understand and respect the mechanisms that guide their operation.

We spend a great deal of time advising sponsors and agents on how to succeed in triangular situations. To sponsors, we offer this guidance: Always endorse the change project with the targets yourself *before* you have the agents actually implement the change. Once employees realize that the boss is supporting a particular change, they are much more likely to cooperate.

To agents, we strongly suggest that they be wary of the risks involved in a project that calls for them to give orders to people who do not report directly to them. In such situations, they may be able to help *facilitate* change, but only after the targets' boss has informed them that he or she supports it.

In the square relationship structure, agents report to one sponsor and targets to another. These relationships are also usually dysfunctional in most organizations. The problems occur when Sponsor One directs his agent to bypass Sponsor Two and go directly to the target to gain compliance for a change. Targets rarely respond to major change directives unless these directives come from their sponsor, who controls the consequences applicable to them. In such situations, Sponsor One and the agent are actually advocates, because they have no power to sanction the change with the targets. We have found that unsuccessful advocates try to directly influence the targets, usually failing because the targets' sponsor does not support the change. For an organization's vice president of budget and finance to have one of his or her financial officers go to the firm's marketing manager to insist on new cost-cutting procedures is not only ineffective but counterproductive. The finance department's best strategy is for the vice president of budget and finance to have his financial officer try to convince the vice president of sales and marketing that the measures are worthy and have her introduce the changes to her people.

Successful advocates spend their time with the sponsors of the targets, engaging in "remedy selling" and "pain management." They help the sponsor realize the importance of the desired change.

11

Project Change Management
Tools and Methodologies

TYPICAL PROJECT CHANGE MANAGEMENT
TOOLS AND USAGE

Projects can be managed skillfully or haphazardly. The following is a list of the innovative change management (ICM) life-cycle phases:

- Phase I—Clarify
- Phase II—Announce
- Phase III—Diagnose
- Phase IV—Plan
- Phase V—Implementation
- Phase VI—Monitor
- Phase VII—Final Evaluation

To be a skillful project manager, the individual must acquire the ability to use a large number of tools effectively. The following is a list of the majority of tools that are in the project manager's armory. The tools with an asterisk (*) behind them of them are project change management (PCM) weapons. Table 11.1 is a list of the 44 most used change management tools and methodologies.

Some of the more commonly used project management tools and techniques (as recommended by the Project Management Institute [PMI] and others) are listed in Table 11.2. We use this table to evaluate the maturity level of the organization's project management team members

The degree of ICM effort is greatly based on the maturity level of the project management team. Mature project management team members

TABLE 11.1

The 44 Most Used Change Management Tools and Methodologies

Managing Organizational Change (MOC) Assessments, Planning Tools, and Training	Pre-Work	Phases						
		I	II	III	IV	V	VI	VII
Change agent evaluation (A)	×			×				
Change agent selection form (A)	×			×				
Change history survey (A)*		×						
Change project description form (P)	×	×	×	×	×	×	×	×
Change resistance scale (A)			×	×				
Communicating change: project analysis (P)			×					
Communicating change: constituency analysis (P)			×					
Communicating change: statement development (P)			×					
Communicating change: announcement plan (P)			×					
Culture assessment (A)				×				
Culture audit (A)				×				
Expectations for a successful change project (A)		×						
Implementation plan advocacy kit (P)					×			
Implementation plan evaluation (A)					×			
Implementation problems assessment (A)				×				
Landscape survey (A)*		×		×		×	×	×
MOC training for sponsors, agents, targets, and advocates (T)	×	×			×			

(Continued)

TABLE 11.1 (Continued)

The 44 Most Used Change Management Tools and Methodologies

Managing Organizational Change (MOC) Assessments, Planning Tools, and Training	Pre-Work	Phases						
		I	II	III	IV	V	VI	VII
Organizational change implementation plan (P)					×	×	×	×
Overload index (A)*		×				×	×	
Pain management strategies: sponsor (P)	×							
Postmortem process**								×
Predicting the impact of change (A)		×						
Preliminary implementation plan (P)					×			
Role map application tool (P)	×	×	×		×	×	×	×
Senior team value for discipline (A)		×						
Sponsor checklist (A)		×		×				
Sponsor evaluation (A)		×		×				
Synergy survey (A)		×		×				
When to apply implementation architecture (A)		×						

Pre-Work—Used before starting Phase I.

* This assessment tool is scored by Organization Development Resource's diagnostic services.

** This project-effectiveness evaluation tool is not MOC specific.

TABLE 11.2

Recommended Tools by the Project Management Institute in *A Guide to the Project Management Body of Knowledge* (PMBOK) Document

PMBOK Tools	Don't Know It	Know It, but Haven't Used It	Used It	Mastered It
1. Arrow diagramming method (ADM)				
2. Benchmarking				
3. Benefit/cost analysis				
4. Bidders' conferences				
5. Bottom-up estimating				
6. Change control system				
7. Checklists				
8. Communications skills				
9. Computerized tools				
10. Conditional diagramming methods				
11. Configuration management				
12. Contingency planning				
13. Contract change control system				
14. Contract type selection				
15. Control charts				
16. Control negotiation				
17. Cost change control system				
18. Cost estimating tools and techniques				
19. Decision trees				
20. Decomposition				
21. Design of experiments				
22. Duration compression				
23. Earned value analysis				
24. Expected monetary value				
25. Expert judgment				
26. Flowcharting				
27. Human resource practices				

(*Continued*)

TABLE 11.2 (*Continued*)

Recommended Tools by the Project Management Institute in *A Guide to the Project Management Body of Knowledge* (PMBOK) Document

PMBOK Tools	Don't Know It	Know It, but Haven't Used It	Used It	Mastered It
28. Independent estimates				
29. Information distribution systems				
30. Information distribution tools and techniques				
31. Information retrieval systems				
32. Interviewing techniques				
33. Make-or-buy analysis				
34. Mathematical analysis				
35. Negotiating techniques				
36. Network templates				
37. Organizational procedures development				
38. Organizational theory				
39. Parametric modeling				
40. Pareto diagrams				
41. Payment system analysis				
42. Performance measurement analysis				
43. Performance reporting tools and techniques				
44. Performance reviews				
45. Preassignment technique				
46. Precedence diagramming method (PDM)				
47. Procurement audits				
48. Product analysis				
49. Product skills and knowledge				
50. Project management information system (PMIS)				
51. PMIS organizational procedures				
52. Project management software				

(*Continued*)

TABLE 11.2 (*Continued*)

Recommended Tools by the Project Management Institute in *A Guide to the Project Management Body of Knowledge* (PMBOK) Document

PMBOK Tools	Don't Know It	Know It, but Haven't Used It	Used It	Mastered It
53. Project management training				
54. Project planning methodology				
55. Project selection methods				
56. Quality audits				
57. Quality planning tools and techniques				
58. Resource leveling heuristics				
59. Reward and recognition systems				
60. Schedule change control system				
61. Scope change control system				
62. Screening system				
63. Simulation modeling				
64. Stakeholder analysis				
65. Stakeholder skills and knowledge				
66. Statistical sampling				
67. Statistical sums				
68. Status review meetings				
69. Team-building activities				
70. Trend analysis				
71. Variance analysis				
72. Weighting system				
73. Work authorization system				
74. Work breakdown structure templates				
75. Workarounds approaches				
Total				
Times weight	0	1	2	3
Point score				

already have a degree of ICM built into their DNA. The following is the point scoring system:

- Mastered it = 3 points
- Used it = 2 points
- Know it, but have not used it = 1 point
- Do not know it = 0 points

Using the sum of the individual points, the following is your project management team members' maturity level:

- Excellent project manager 175–200
- Acceptable project manager 125–174
- Acceptable project team member 100–124
- Unacceptable project manager 50–99
- Unacceptable project team member 0–49

Any project manager who has a point score below 125 needs project management training.

PROJECT MANAGEMENT LIFE CYCLE

The project management life cycle is divided into six phases. (The project management life cycle will vary based on the complexity of the project.)

- Phase I—Selection (project business case)
- Phase II—Initiation (develop charter and have a project manager assign)
- Phase III—Planning (requirements, scope, work breakdown structure)
- Phase IV—Execution (design, development, and schedule)
- Phase V—Control (reviews and metrics)
- Phase VI—Closure (administrative and contractual to marry)

Table 11.3 shows how the seven PCM phases relate to the six project phases.

Table 11.4 shows the relationship between the phases of an environmental management systems implementation and typical PCM activities.

TABLE 11.3

Comparison of the Seven PCM Phases to the Six Project Phases

Seven PCM Phases	Phase I: Concept and Definition	Phase II: Design and Development	Phase III: Creating the Product or Service	Phase IV: Installation and Maintenance	Phase V: Operating	Phase VI: Disposal
Phase I—Clarify	■					
Phase II—Announce		■				
Phase III—Diagnose		■				
Phase IV—Plan		■	■			
Phase V—Implement			■	■		
Phase VI—Monitor				■	■	
Phase VII—Final Evaluation					■	■

TABLE 11.4

Relationship between the Six Phases of an EMS Implementation and Typical PCM Activities

Typical PCM Activities

Keyed to EMS Phases in Project

PCM Activities	Phase 1: Assess	Phase 2: Plan	Phase 3: Redesign	Phase 4: Implement	Phase 5: Audit	Phase 6: Improve
Identify, document, and communicate cost of the status quo (business imperative)	▮			▮		
Create and communicate the future state vision (people, process, and technology)	▮					
Clarify the change and obtain initiating sponsor understanding and commitment	▮					
Create needed infrastructure and implementation architecture						
Conduct a high-level quality management system–wide change risk assessment (the eight risk factors)			▮			
Create a high-level organizational change plan						
Create role maps to identify all personnel having key change roles		▮		▮		
Conduct tier-level change risk assessments (the eight risk factors)						
Conduct change readiness assessments						
Organizational alignment assessment (structure, compensation, rewards, etc.)	▮					
Assess enablers and barriers						
Develop tier-level transition management plans						

(*Continued*)

TABLE 11.4 (*Continued*)

Relationship between the Six Phases of an EMS Implementation and Typical PCM Activities

Typical PCM Activities

Keyed to EMS Phases in Project

PCM Activities	Phase 1: Assess	Phase 2: Plan	Phase 3: Redesign	Phase 4: Implement	Phase 5: Audit	Phase 6: Improve
Develop a communication plan						
Cascade sponsorship (communications, training, performance management)			█			
Implement the communication plan			█	█	█	█
Provide change management training for sponsors, change agents, and others			█	█		
Form change agent, sponsor, and advocate teams			█	█	█	█
Provide training for targets (those affected by the change)			█	█		
Implement organizational alignment enablers						
Analyze effectiveness of communications and training strategies						
Monitor commitment levels of sponsors, change agents, advocates, and targets						█
Monitor and measure implementation effectiveness and schedule adherence					█	█
Modify transition management plans as needed to assure effectiveness						
Track and report planned versus actual activities and results					█	█
Identify opportunities for continuous improvement to the change process						█

It is evident from Table 11.4 that a number of PCM activities are iterative in nature and are not confined to one environmental management systems (EMS) phase. In reality, PCM becomes part of the way projects are managed. It is an important management factor because cost, quality, and schedule are all affected negatively if the change process is poorly managed.

12

Setting the Stage for Project Change Management

THE CHANGE PROCESS

Bringing about change in an organization should be considered a process. Like any other process, the starting point is what we call the "status quo" or AS/IS status. At this step in the process, it is relatively a stable process that the employees have become familiar with and are confident that they can perform at a level that is acceptable to management. They may not like everything that is going on, but they are familiar with it and feel comfortable with it (see Figure 12.1). The changes being made impact the individual as the status quo is disrupted and the process moves on to the transition state. The transition state is a very unstable state because the outcome usually is unclear and how it will impact the employee is not understood. For example, this change could result in job loss, lower pay, changing locations, and so on.

The last activity in the change process is when the change has been implemented and the future state is now the designated operating mode. All too frequently, the future state, once it has been implemented, does not measure up to the promises that were given to management and the employees. Also, for every positive change there often is an unexpected negative impact on the improvement initiative. Figure 12.2 shows the change process with three key enablers added to the change process chart:

1. Pain drivers
2. Implementation architecture
3. Future state vision

These three key enablers are required to make the process function.

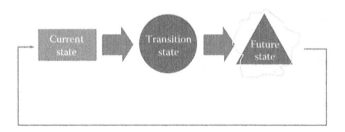

FIGURE 12.1
Change is a process.

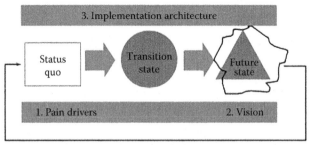

FIGURE 12.2
The change process with three of the key items added to it.

Actions to clarify the cost of the status quo for the stakeholders are as follows:

- Cost/benefit analysis
- Open, honest management
- Business imperative analysis
- Industry benchmarking
- Cost of quality audit
- Customer survey
- Past history surveys
- Value analysis
- Business case analysis
- Industry trend analysis
- Audit management letter
- Force field analysis
- Current state assessment
- Future state clarification

It is pretty obvious to people that the stress of a rapidly changing organization can be difficult and unpleasant. What's not so clear to us sometimes is how much trouble we're in if the organization fails to change.

Price Pritchett
The Employee Handbook for Organizational Change

A STRUCTURED APPROACH TO PROJECT CHANGE MANAGEMENT

Organizations need to manage change utilizing a structured approach. To help visualize the process structure, we can use the block diagram shown in Figure 12.3.

Individual Project Change Management Methodology Plan

The change facilitator will prepare a specific part of the project plan that will be referred to as the project change management (PCM) plan. In addition, the change facilitator will input PCM requirements into the following parts of the project plan:

- Project integration management
- Project time management

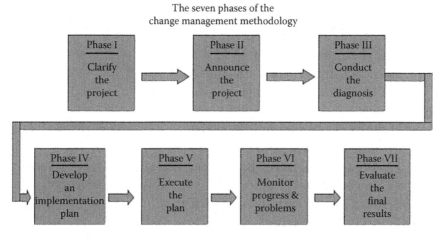

FIGURE 12.3
Change management flowchart.

- Project cost management
- Project quality management
- Project human resource management
- Project communication management
- Project risk management

The PCM plan will include the following:

- Timing and scope of all PCM assessments that will be conducted
- Degree of acceptance of the project's output that is required by the organization and the targeted individuals
- PCM training plans
- Target plus-minus analysis and communication approach
- Project impact strategy
- PCM roles and responsibilities of all project team members and impacted organizations
- Timeline chart of PCM activities
- Definitions of integration dependencies

PCM Implementation Plan

The challenge that faces the change facilitator and the rest of the project team is to implement all of the individual sections that make up the project plan and still meet the cost, schedule, and performance requirements. For the change facilitator, it involves activities such as the following:

- Conducting assessments
- Attending project reviews
- Developing target plus-minus analysis
- Communicating project objectives and visions
- Communicating with the targets
- Defining required commitment levels
- Managing resistance to the project
- Ensuring that the targets have an excellent vision of how the project will impact them
- Building commitment to the project
- Ensuring that the targets' concerns are considered
- Ensuring that suggestions made by the targets are acted on and that the people who made the suggestions get feedback and credit

The PCM activities are some of the first activities that should get under-way in a project. Just ask yourself, "At my organization, how long does it take for the rumor mill to spread a story like 'Management is reengi-neering our jobs and 80% of us will be laid off.'" We don't know about your specific organization, but at most of the organizations we work with, it does not take weeks, or even days, and in many of them, not even hours. The rumor mill spreads out these juicy bits of false informa-tion in minutes. Even before a decision can be reached whether or not to reengineer a process, the rumor mill will have many people upset. These rumors set in place a momentum that, if not checked, will be detrimental to the success of the project. As a result, the PCM activities must start long before the project team takes the time to document a project plan. Often, these activities need to continue long after the proj-ect has been implemented.

The Seven PCM Support Patterns

The following is a list of support patterns that we have found useful in applying PCM to projects. These are the key elements of the Landscape Survey.

- *Support Pattern 1: The Nature of Change*
  Why major change is difficult to assimilate
  Control: The extent to which respondents feel they are unable to control what happens to them (direct control) or anticipate the sequence of events (indirect control)
  Microlevel Impact: The extent to which individuals do not perceive the change as having an impact on their day-to-day activities
  Assimilation Capacity: The extent to which individuals do not have an adequate level of personal resources to deal with the demands presented by change
- *Support Pattern 2: The Process of Change*
  The key elements and the flow of events involved in human transition
  Pain: The extent to which individuals fail to see the status quo as leading to either problems or missed opportunities
  Desired State: The extent to which the targets are unable to envi-sion the way things are supposed to be once the change is fully implemented

Remedy: The extent to which individuals fail to acknowledge the value of the specific change being implemented

Architecture: The extent to which respondents fail to recognize a workable plan to move from the status quo to the desired state

- *Support Pattern 3: The Roles of Change*

  The roles that are central to change in organizational settings

  Initiating Sponsorship: Inadequate support from those persons who initially sanction the change

  Sustaining Sponsorship: Inadequate support from those persons who sanction the change at local levels within the organization

  Agent Capability: Inadequate level of skill possessed by those persons who are responsible for change implementation

- *Support Pattern 4: Resistance of Change*

  How and why resistance forms

  Willingness: The extent to which the change is incongruent with respondents' goals and values

  Ability: The extent to which respondents do not perceive that they possess the skills and abilities needed to accomplish the change

- *Support Pattern 5: Commitment to Change*

  The sequence of events involved in people becoming committed to a change

  Commitment: The extent to which the respondents' level of commitment to the change does not match the level needed for the change to succeed

- *Support Pattern 6: Culture and Change*

  Why organizational culture is so important to the success of a change

  Cultural Consistency: The degree to which the beliefs, behaviors, and assumptions required by the change are inconsistent with those currently in existence

  Change History: The extent to which respondents currently hold negative expectations, based on their experience with previous changes, about the organization's capacity for implementing change

- *Support Pattern 7: Synergy and Change*

  Why powerful teamwork is at the heart of achieving change objectives

  Common Goals: The extent to which targets do not see themselves as working toward a clear, shared goal in the change

Interdependence: The extent to which targets do not recognize the necessity of working collaboratively with coworkers to accomplish the change

Empowerment: Perceptions by the targets that their contributions regarding the change are not valued or influential

Participative Management: The extent to which managers fail to seek the highest appropriate levels of input from targets regarding the change

Synergy Skills: The extent to which respondents do not use the skills necessary for synergistic interaction in the change process

INNOVATIVE CHANGE MANAGEMENT APPROACH APPLIED TO A COMPLEX PROJECT

The following is a list of tasks that would typically be undertaken when innovative change management is applied to a complex project:

- Project start-up and preparation
- Initiate project
- Define project charter
- Clarify scope of organizational change
- Develop project plan
- Review and approve project charter and project plan
- Kick off the project
- Current people infrastructure description
  - Describe the current organizational environment
- Define current change management process
- Review and approve current people infrastructure stage
- Enterprise people infrastructure definition
  - Define people enablement framework
  - Review and approve enterprise people infrastructure stage
- Pilot planning
  - Assess change management enablers and barriers
- Define pilot phase strategies
- Develop pilot phase transition management plan
- Develop initial pilot phase schedule

- Develop initial project charters—pilot
- Review and approve pilot planning stage
- Transition management
  - Refine transition enablers and barriers assessment
  - Refine transition management infrastructure
  - Develop transition management plan
  - Review and approve transition management stage
- Future state design
  - Perform people enabler detailed analysis
  - Define people enabler design
  - Review and approve future state design stage
- People enabler development
  - Develop people enablers
  - Review and approve staff training stage development
- Training development
  - Develop training program
  - Prepare for training
  - Review and approve training development stage
- Business case refinement
  - Conduct cost/benefit analysis
  - Analyze risk and return
  - Review and approve pilot business case refinement stage
- Implementation planning
- Develop implementation plan
- Develop initial project charters—implementation
- Review and approve implementation planning stage
- Communications management
- Implement communication plan
- Develop communications status report
- Conduct change communication intervention
- Refine implementation management infrastructure
- Review and approve communications management stage
- Staff training
  - Conduct training
- Review and approve staff training stage
- Change implementation monitoring
  - Track and monitor enablers and barriers management plan
  - Review and approve change implementation monitoring stage

- Evolution planning
  - Verify business value
  - Identify evolution options
  - Develop evolution vision
  - Develop evolution plan
  - Review and approve evolution planning stage
- Project review and assessment
  - Review project performance
  - Close down project

In reality, PCM becomes part of the way projects are managed and becomes as important a management factor as cost, quality, and schedule, because they are all affected if the change process is poorly managed.

PCM AND PROJECT MANAGEMENT WORKING TOGETHER

PCM is a critical project management skill that must be part of all major project management initiatives. Not having PCM plans integrated into the project plan greatly increases the risk related to not completing the project on schedule, completing within budget, and providing an output that is not valued by the customer. PCM is the tenth ingredient in the project management toolbox.

> It is inadequate to manage just project cost, schedule, and quality. Without managing the project's social impact, most projects will fail to reach their full potential.

How PCM Fits into Project Management Methodology

It is imperative that the PCM activities are integrated and completely aligned with the project management activities. This is accomplished by making the PCM plan part of the project management plan. Then, involve as many of the project management team members in implementing the PCM plan as possible.

Project managers must be as skilled and familiar with PCM concepts as they are with financial management. In fact, the skills that the project managers have related to PCM often have a much greater impact on the outcome of the project than financial controls. The degree and amount of resistance to change impacts cost, schedule, resource requirements, and the performance of the end output from the project. No longer can project managers limit their project design to just the resources consumed by the project. An effective project management plan needs to prepare the targets (the people who need to change) so that the results of the project will be effectively assimilated into the organization. Too often, project managers look at the four key project management factors—process, knowledge, technology, and people—and limit their people's thinking to the make-up of the project team. As a result, the project team is made up of technology experts who have little or no knowledge or concern related to the people who are impacted by the project and have to live with the project results day after day.

The project manager must be skilled at

- Being a change agent
- Being a change advocate
- Being a change facilitator
- Being a change target

PCM RISK FACTORS

Figure 12.4 is a picture of the eight change management risk factors that we discuss.

As you entered the PCM installation's cycle, there are many risks that need to be faced and controlled. The following lists eight of these risks that the change management team frequently has to address:

1. Cost of the status quo
2. Vision clarity
3. Sponsor's commitment
4. Change agent/advocacy skills
5. Target response
6. Culture/organizational alignment
7. Internal and external organizational events
8. Implementation architecture

Eight implementation/human
project risk factors

FIGURE 12.4
PCM risk factors.

PCM Risk Factor #1: Cost of the Status Quo

We all complain about the way things are (i.e., how early we have to get up to go to work, the lack of parking places in the garage, Tim is always late with this report, my boss is too busy to spend time with me, etc.). But still we don't really want to see him change from, "My boss is too busy to spend time with me" to "He tried to tell me exactly how to do everything." Yes, we all recognize problems with the status quo (i.e., too much paperwork, poor staff attitude, too little pay, too much bureaucracy in our processes, the coffee is cold as it comes out of the machine, etc.). Certainly, the status quo conditions are never perfect, but we are masters of our own fate, and as a result of our blood, sweat, and tears, we believe we are the best-trained and knowledgeable individual to do the job we are doing. We have a great deal of pride and satisfaction in the status quo, as well as a few things to complain about. There are four parts of pain related to the status quo:

- Current problems
- Anticipated problems
- Anticipated opportunities
- Current opportunities

Status Quo Pain Drivers

The situation can be represented by a 2×2 matrix (see Figure 12.5).

A. Status quo *current problem pain*—problem-related pain (upper left-hand box)
   - *Situation*: "We're in trouble now."
   - *Pain driver*: The immediate loss of our market dominance, job security, organizational survival, etc.

   Current problem pain is the pain of the individual who would be impacted by the proposed change (target) if it was implemented. It is a pain that the impacted people understand as they live with it every day. It is usually a pain that management does not understand and is often not interested in no matter what they say. Unfortunately, this type of pain varies from job to job and often from individual to individual within a job. All too often, this type of pain is not documented or considered. It is a type of pain that results in high turnover in an organization. It is too bad that many of the focus groups that have employees on them concentrate on "What the change will do for them," rather than asking the question "What should we do to correct the pain you're having today?" There's a song in the movie *Chicago* that goes something like this: "You do something good for mommy and mommy will do something

People are willing to pay the price for solving a problem or capturing an opportunity.

	Problem	Opportunity
Current	Situation: "We're in trouble now."	Situation: "If we act immediately, we can take advantage of this situation."
Anticipated	Situation: "We're going to be in trouble."	Situation: "In the future, we could be in a position to profit from what is going to happen."

FIGURE 12.5
Status quo pain drivers.

good for you." This is a small part of a PCM process. Start off your focus group by listing the conditions that your emplolyees would like to change, and be sure that they are addressed in the final change proposal.

B. Status quo *current opportunity pain*—this is the pain that would be created if you don't change pain (upper right-hand box)

- *Situation*: "If we act immediately, we can take advantage of this situation."
- *Pain driver*: The loss of a potential advantage that is within our grasp

    Current opportunity pain is change that takes advantage of a specific opportunity that often needs to be addressed in the short range in order to take advantage of the opportunity. For example, I was recently looking for a new car, and I saw exactly what I would like to get in a crossover Chevrolet with heated seats. It was on sale for $3000 under suggested Blue Book price. I wanted to trade in a car that I hadn't driven for over 6 months. I went home to get the car so they could appraise it, and the battery was dead. By the time we got a new battery and installed it, was almost 6 pm, and so we decided to go to the car dealership the following day. We got there at about 2 pm only to find out that the car I wanted had been sold. I had a current opportunity but didn't take advantage of it in an expeditious manner, and as a result, I am still driving my old car.

    Another example: Company A has received complaints that some customers feel the screen on their cell phones is too small. We now have the technology that allows us to make the screen 1.5 inches bigger. When we were preparing the value proposition and the pilot run, our competition came out with a screen that was bigger than our current screen, and they walked away with the market. It was a good opportunity, but we reacted too slowly to take advantage of it.

    These are opportunities that usually management, research and development, and sales and marketing discover. It is seldom that these types of opportunities are brought to management's attention by the people who are impacted by the change initiative. Management has the responsibility to bring these types of opportunities to everyone's attention so that a sense of urgency can be established.

C. Status quo *anticipated opportunities pain* (lower right-hand box)
- *Situation*: "We're going to be in trouble."
- *Pain driver*: The impending loss of our market dominance, job security, organizational survival, etc.

  Anticipated opportunities are the events that possibly could happen that would be beneficial to one or more stakeholders. For example, if we could build a rocket ship that would take us to outer space and return to an airfield undamaged, there would be an opportunity to sell many tickets at $1 million a piece. Anticipated opportunities are ones that we cannot take advantage of now and will have to invest in to develop the technology or the product before we can benefit from it. These are concepts that typically come from customers, sales and marketing, research and development, and management. Using the targets of the change management are not the individuals who identify anticipated opportunities.

D. Status quo *anticipated problem pain* (lower left-hand box)
- *Situation*: "In the future we could be in a position to profit from what is going to happen."
- *Pain driver*: The loss of a potential advantage that is possible to achieve in the future.

Current opportunities can provide added value to one or more of the stakeholders. On occasion, they provide a negative impact on some of the stakeholders. For example, the organization could plan on moving manufacturing from San Jose, California, to Shanghai, China. This would reduce manufacturing cost by 15%. This change action should have a positive impact on the profit for the organization and on the dividends paid to the investors. It would have a very negative impact on the manufacturing workers who would lose their jobs. This information is not usually discussed openly, other than in the management ranks.

It is interesting to note that of the four pain drivers, the status quo environment is the only one of them that is not visible to the people impacted by the change prior to the change being made. As a result, when we talk about pain related to the status quo, management has to obtain a crisp understanding of the three "what if we don't change" conditions and honestly share that information with the individuals who are impacted by the change. Typically, the pain related to current problem pain is a very small portion of the pain related to the status quo if it is not changed. In most cases, management action never steps up to correct the current problem pain as viewed from the people who are impacted by the change.

We recommend making a pain list with the following headings:

- Current problems
- Anticipated problems
- Anticipated opportunities
- Current opportunities

Under each of the four headings, the program manager, project manager, and change manager should make a list of the potential problems and opportunities that the current process is faced with. This usually is the start of the risk management part of the project plan. As part of the business case analysis, the proposed solution should be compared to this list to identify the problems and opportunities that the proposed project will not correct.

PCM Risk Factor #2: Vision Clarity

In Figure 12.6, vision clarity is rated as the number 2 impact area. This is when the individuals, who would be impacted by the change, understand the negative and positive impacts of the change on the status quo situation for the organization. In most cases, a fairly negative picture of the status

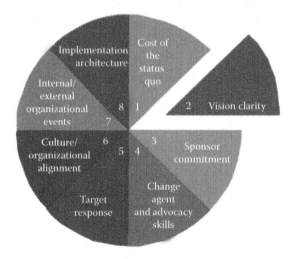

FIGURE 12.6
Risk factor 2: vision clarity.

quo has been brought to the attention of the targeted audience. Now we have to offset this with a very positive understanding of what impact the change will have on the problems, the employee, and opportunities related to the status quo. This means that we should generate an understanding in the employee's mind related to how the change is going to impact him or her. Most organizations believe that developing a vision statement is adequate to do this job. We believe that the vision statement is about 20% of the total effort that is needed to provide the employees with a clear view of the future after the change is implemented.

It's like I'm riding in my new gold-colored Jaguar XKE down the winding road traveling 110 miles an hour (see Figure 12.7). It had been raining and my windows were covered with mud, so I couldn't see where I was going. I didn't know if I should turn left, turn right, or go straight ahead. Management needs to provide the impacted people with an excellent understanding of where they are going and how they are going to get there. A well-thought-out paragraph describing the future conditions is a good start, but it does not fulfill the employees' needs. What we need to do is to provide our employees with both visual and verbal understanding of the future environment and how they will personally relate to it. You cannot get by having a meeting and explaining it to them. It needs to be reinforced over and over again to the point that when they shut their eyes, they can see the future. For example, when I was working for Ernst & Young, we acquired three rooms to demonstrate this to one of our clients. In the first room, we set up a model of the AS/IS state. In the second room, we set up a model of how the organization would be operating 6 months in the future. In the third room, we set up a simulation of how they would be operating when the project would be completely installed. We took the executive team into each of these three large rooms explaining what was

Get a clear view of
where you need to go

FIGURE 12.7
Get a clear view.

going on and how things would change from the AS/IS model. We also walked thought-leader-type employees through the three rooms, carefully noting their comments and suggestions. We could not install the software required for the completed assignment. So, we had an individual behind the scenes manipulating the data as though the software packages were installed and working.

PAIN MANAGEMENT

If the change targets do not personally feel that there is more pain related to the status quo than the pain they will experience going through the transitional period plus the pain that they will have when the future state initiative is implemented, they will fight tooth and nail to shoot it down. Remember that you cannot explain pain from the organization's standpoint. Pain is personal and must be addressed from the individual standpoint.

TRANSITION

So far, we have discussed everything in Figure 12.2 except transition. We talked about the *status quo* so we know where we are, and we talked about the future state (*vision*) so we know where we are going. Now we need to sit down and think about what we are going to do to connect the two together. Let's look at an example. I live in Los Gatos, California, and I thoroughly understand the stress related to living here. In Los Gatos, there is too much traffic; housing is overpriced in most areas, driving the price of a small three bedroom home up into the million dollar range; the squirrels eat all my flowers; my water bill runs over $400 a month; and it costs $108 an hour to have a mechanic fix my car. Where I really want to live is in Hawaii, so I dream about it nightly. I have been in Hawaii three times and am scheduled to go again in July. We always go to the same spot and stay in a three-bedroom oceanfront house. It is so close that I could almost spit from the porch into the water. My granddaughter loves to play in the sand, and you cannot get my daughter-in-law out of the water. There are two tall palm trees right in front of the porch. The pool is no more than 50 feet away from us. I am sitting here in Los Gatos at 7 pm with my eyes closed, and the picture in my mind is so real I could almost count the blades of grass. We have the status quo and the crisp vision of where we want to go. Now all we need to do is go through the transition of moving the family from Los Gatos to Hawaii. We have already started the planning for the transition. A friend of mine had a 35-foot sailboat that he has agreed to let us borrow. This is a very simple transition. You get on board the boat in Los Gatos, and the wind will move you along directly to Hawaii, or maybe it isn't that simple. Here's where the four C's come in:

- Competency—I've never sailed even a little boat. My wife is afraid of water because she doesn't know how to swim, and she plans on staying down below in the cabin for the whole trip. I know how to read a compass, but I have never used one to get from one place to another.
- Comfort—I was in the Navy, but every time we put out to sea I got very seasick. I used to walk around the deck carrying a bucket that I would throw up into.
- Confidence—Without knowing how to use a compass to steer by, we are liable to end up in New Zealand or on some deserted island where we would be eaten by some cannibals.
- Control—A friend tells me that he does not have a radio on the sailboat because all he does is sail around in the San Francisco Bay. If I get into trouble, I don't know how I'm going to reach AAA (American Automobile Association) to get help.

If you are depending on the wind to provide the energy to move the boat, how can you be sure that the wind will be blowing in the right direction or even if there will be a wind to blow in any direction?

Now I admit this is an extreme example, but it is very close to how the impacted people feel about the transitional period. They are entering into a sea of unknown that someone else controls—our future. They do not even know who that someone else is. They have been told that this mysterious someone was going to make things better for them. What the employees are really thinking is, "Show me, and then I will believe." We all hope and usually base our projections on the belief that the wind will be constant and the sea calm. What really happens is we are halfway to Hawaii and a typhoon strikes the Pacific Ocean.

OTHER PCM RISK FACTORS

We already discussed two out of the eight PCM risk factors—cost of the status quo and vision clarity as shown in Figure 12.4. The following is a very short review of the other risk factors as shown in Figure 12.8:

- Risk 3. Sponsor's commitment
- Risk 4. Change agent/advocacy skills
- Risk 5. Target response
- Risk 6. Culture/organizational alignment
- Risk 7. Internal and external organizational events
- Risk 8. Implementation architecture

PCM Risk Factor #3: Sponsor's Commitment

Change management is a very difficult skill to master. It's easy to get up and give a speech or go to a seminar or put out a memo, but basically leading change is a day-to-day activity that takes a lot of work, a lot of energy.

Mark Huselid
Author, The HR Scorecard

FIGURE 12.8
Risk factors 3 through 8.

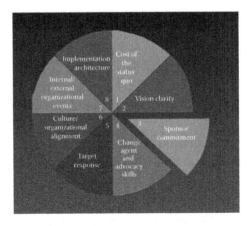

FIGURE 12.9
Risk factor 3: sponsor commitment.

Figure 12.9 shows the sponsor commitment as the third item in the eight risk factors. In change management, we have two kinds of sponsors—sustaining sponsor and initiating sponsor. The sustaining sponsor is responsible for identifying targets within their assigned span of control, understanding the target's role in the change process, and working with the targets to break down any resistance that they may have to the change. They play a major role in communicating the project's vision, mission, and objectives to the targets. They also help to develop an understanding of the pain related to the present-state and anticipated future-state solutions.

PCM Risk Factor #4: Change Agent/Advocacy Skills

Today, change agents must be facilitators of the human aspects of change.

H. J. Harrington

Change agents are very special people. They have to have excellent people skills and be able to understand and interpret their behavioral patterns. These are individuals who until recently were not part of most project teams. The project manager often plays the role of the change agent without the required training. Basically, the change agent is responsible for making the change happen. The key attributes of an effective change agent include the following:

- Work within expectations set by the sponsor
- Apply in-depth understanding of how people and organizations react to the process of change

- Value the human as well as the technical aspects of change
- Identify, relate to, and respect the different viewpoints of sponsors, agents, and targets
- Collect and appropriately use data regarding how and why people will resist change
- Help build and maintain synergy among sponsors, agents, and targets
- Communicate effectively with a broad range of people with different communication styles
- Help build and maintain appropriate levels of commitment to the change throughout the change-implementation process
- Use his or her power and influence to achieve the goals of the change
- Set aside personal agendas, desires, and biases that might hinder the success of the project
- Be very effective and proficient at using all the change management tools

It is very important to select excellent change agents, and they should be evaluated after each project based on the following:

- Is the individual perceived as highly credible?
- Has the individual earned the sponsor's trust and respect?
- Does the individual demonstrate a high tolerance for ambiguity?
- Does the individual thrive on challenge while avoiding stress levels associated with burnout?
- Is the individual aware of the formal and informal power structure and know how to use it?
- Does the individual have a good understanding of change management concepts and principles?
- Does the individual have a high level of political support and credibility?
- Can the individual effectively manage ambiguity and uncertainty?
- Can the individual work within the sponsor's expectations?

Individuals who have the personal traits to be change agents should be trained on the change management methodology. If the individual does not have the necessary personal traits, select another individual. It takes a long time to develop the needed personal traits.

PCM Risk Factor #5: Target Response

Anyone affected by the change is a target. If the president of an organization is the initiating sponsor of a project to install a new labor-claiming system that will be used by all the research engineers, the vice president of research and development is a target who must be convinced that it is good for him or her. The president has the responsibility to convince the vice president of research and development that it is good for his or her organization to the point that the vice president converts from a target and becomes a sustaining sponsor. However, just because the vice president becomes a sustaining sponsor, it does not mean that he or she is no longer a target. Quite the contrary, he or she will always remain a target that the president must keep dealing with to be sure that he or she does not have any doubts about the value of the projects the organization has undertaken.

Targets must be educated to understand that they are expected to accommodate change. They must be involved appropriately in the design and implementation process if they are going to embrace the change. Too many people think that targets are people who just sit there and have changes imposed upon them. They believe that they have no responsibility for ensuring that the change is successful. That may have been the case some time ago when a successful project, from the target's standpoint, was one that they could say, "See. I told you it would not work."

Today the targets take on a key responsibility of providing input into the design that reflects the real operating environment. There is nothing like experience in doing the actual job to define flaws in a software or process design. The targets have the responsibility to maintain an open mind, to give constructive suggestions, and to help with the implementation.

> Only those who constantly retool themselves stand a chance of staying employed in the years ahead.
>
> **Tom Peters**

Good targets not only embrace change, they make it happen.

PCM Risk Factor #6: Culture/Organizational Alignment

Individual projects that are based on changing the organization's culture are doomed to failure. Organizational culture change takes years

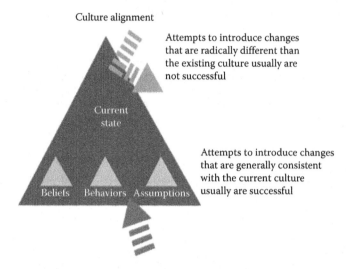

Culture alignment

Attempts to introduce changes that are radically different than the existing culture usually are not successful

Current state

Attempts to introduce changes that are generally consistent with the current culture usually are successful

Beliefs   Behaviors   Assumptions

FIGURE 12.10
Cultural impact on projects.

to become embedded in an organization. Projects that are not in line with the present organization's culture have a very high risk of failure (see Figure 12.10). You have two options if the project is not in line with the organization's culture:

- Modifying the project so that it is in line with current culture
- Preparing for the project to fail

PCM Risk Factor #7: Internal and External Organizational Events

Often, many of the largest project management risks are not controllable by the project team. For example, if we went to war, you probably would be building tanks, not cars. If your competition decides to move manufacturing to China, you may have to move your manufacturing activity to Asia or Mexico in order to stay competitive. A new computer chip is released that is 100 times faster and 10% cheaper than the one you are using. Research and development comes up with a new product that makes the one you are working on completely obsolete.

The project team and the change management group need to be continuously monitoring internal and external changes that are taking place and adjusting the plan in accordance with these activities. A great deal of time and money is lost when an organization launches a new product that the competition has already made obsolete.

PCM Risk Factor #8: Implementation Architecture

Figure 12.11 highlights the last risk factor—implementation architecture. The targeted audience can have an excellent understanding of the status quo pain, and when they close their eyes, they can clearly see into their future, its projections, and promises related to the future. You have set very high expectations in the employees' imaginations. It is now up to the management team and project team to deliver on these expectations. It is the implementation architecture that delivers the results and makes the changes. All too many people are good planners, but poor doers. Others just want to do something, no matter what it is, or even if they do not understand what they are doing. They make a lot of noise and accomplish very little.

> Change only occurs when individuals make a choice to change. We have to establish with people that there is less pain in moving.

> **William Bridges**
> *Managing Transitions*

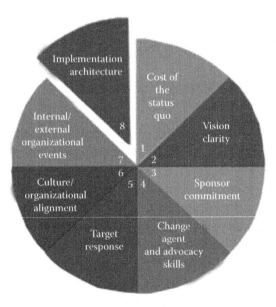

FIGURE 12.11
Risk factor 8: implementation architecture.

Building implementation architecture requires a good understanding of the important leverage points in the implementation process. This includes the use of a structured, yet flexible, framework that uses concepts, techniques, and tools to address factors typically associated with change implementation.

WHEN TO USE PCM

PCM was a real breakthrough in improving the percentage of projects that produce real value added to the organization and customers. They account for between 20% and 30% improvement over previous project management methodologies. The priority for most executive teams is focused on cultural change. Applying PCM concepts to individual projects is inexpensive and effective, if it is done correctly. The problem is that only a small percentage of the total population is affected by the PCM methodology. An estimated 5%–10% of employees are involved in a formal PCM initiative for approximately 30–60 days, and then they are not involved or have an opportunity to use the PCM methodologies for 3–5 years. Even then, not all approved projects use the PCM methodology as part of their work breakdown structure. PCM should be used under the following conditions:

1. When the project is a major undertaking (see Figure 12.12)
2. When there is a high cost if the implementation fails

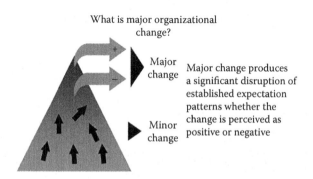

FIGURE 12.12
Selecting the projects that will have a formal PCM methodology applied to them.

3. When there is a high risk that certain human factors could result in implementation failure
4. When the project outcome is not in line with the organization's culture

Organizations start numerous projects with the hopes that one of them will turn out to be successful and lead the organization to the next-generation product. The time to stop a project that is going to fail is before you start it.

13

Summary

TACTICAL AREAS OF RISK IN PROJECT IMPLEMENTATION

First Tactical Risk Area: Sponsor Commitment

When project sponsors do not fully understand a project's implications or are unwilling or unable to take the necessary action, the project manager tries to convince the sponsors that the project is important to the organization. The project manager should be in a position to have the initiating sponsor replaced with someone who will provide the needed support or be prepared for the project to fail.

Without the appropriate project sponsor's attention, energy, action, and other resources, a major project will falter after it is announced. If a sponsor believes the project is a business imperative, he or she will probably be highly committed. If the project sponsor understands how the project will affect the organization, including both its short- and long-term consequences, and can empathize with those impacted directly by the project, he or she will likely sustain this commitment.

A committed project sponsor recognizes the demand that a change project makes on organizational resources, including knowledge, time, and money. The resolute sponsor will also publicly commit these resources while privately meeting with key individuals or groups to convey his or her resolve to see the project succeed. Part of the project manager's role in managing the change requires the project manager to help a sponsor develop reward structures for those who support the implementation and enforce consequences for those who undermine it.

The project manager should assist a sponsor in showing he or she means business by establishing procedures for tracking the progress and problems of a change project. A strong sponsor is aware that personal, political, or organizational costs always accompany major change, and he or she is willing to pay the price. A committed sponsor sacrifices other attractive opportunities if they pose a threat to the original goal. The committed sponsor understands that follow-up is a crucial final step for any successful change project.

One of the ICM roles that the project manager plays is to define and elicit effective sponsor characteristics and behaviors:

- **Power:** The organizational power to legitimize the change with those individuals (targets) whose behavior must change as a result of the project
- **Pain:** A level of discomfort with the status quo that makes change attractive
- **Vision:** A clear definition of what change must occur
- **Resources:** A thorough understanding of the organizational resources (e.g., time, money, and people) necessary for a successful project implementation and the ability and willingness to commit them
- **The long view:** A total, in-depth understanding of the effect the project will have on the organization
- **Sensitivity:** The capacity to fully appreciate and empathize with the personal issues major change raises
- **Scope:** The capacity to understand thoroughly the size of the group to be affected by the project
- **Public role:** The ability and willingness to demonstrate the public support necessary to convey strong organizational commitment to the project
- **Private role:** The ability and willingness to meet privately with key individuals or groups to convey strong personal support for the project
- **Consequence management techniques:** Prepared to promptly reward those who facilitate acceptance of the project or express displeasure with those who inhibit it
- **Monitoring plans:** The determination to ensure that monitoring procedures are established that will track both the transition's progress and problems
- **A willingness to sacrifice:** The commitment to pursue the transition, knowing that a price will most often accompany the project
- **Persistence:** The capacity to demonstrate consistent support for the project and reject any short-term action that is inconsistent with long-term project goals

Obviously, the demands of being a successful sponsor mean that no one can sponsor more than a few major change projects at a time. Yet poor sponsors often engage in far too many change initiatives, draining their time and energy to the point of being unable to adequately perform their duties. The project manager should advise the initiating sponsor of any risks he or she sees in the identified list of cascading sponsors required to sustain the project implementation.

Conducting human due diligence is gathering information, planning, and engaging in actions related to the impact that change is having or will have on an organization's human capital. This includes conducting due diligence to determine if the project is a candidate for an official PCM initiative. This due diligence is normally conducted as part of the business case presentation. In some critical high-return potential projects, a project manager and a change manager may be assigned after successful completion of the value proposition acceptance. This helps the team develop a sound analysis to present to the executive team during the business case analysis.

The only failure is one you didn't learn something from.

H. J. Harrington

Walt Disney rakes in billions from merchandise, movies, and theme parks around the world, but Walt Disney himself had a bit of a rough start. He was fired by a newspaper editor because, "he lacked imagination and had no good ideas." After that, he started a number of businesses that did not last too long and ended with bankruptcy and failure. He kept plugging along (working hard), however, and eventually found a recipe for success that worked.

Section V

Cultural Change Management (CCM)

14

Culture Change Management Introduction

INTRODUCTION TO CULTURE CHANGE MANAGEMENT

Culture change management (CCM) is a slow process that brings about a gradual change in an organization's ability to handle change initiatives without disrupting the organization's performance. It focuses on changing the organization's frame of reference (FOR), making the organization more resilient.

Definitions:

- **Frame of reference (FOR)**—a compatible set of ideas, theories, beliefs, feelings, values, and assumptions that are applied to a person's experience. The frame of reference is an unconscious model comprehending reality.
- **Resilience**—the ability to absorb high levels of disruptive change while displaying minimal dysfunctional behavior. The five characteristics of resilience are positive, focused, proactive, organized, and flexible.
- **Dysfunctional**—any change, related action, or feeling that diverts resources away from meeting productivity and quality standards.
- **Personality**—The way an individual or organization reacts to other individuals or organizations. This outward behavior is based on how the individual or organization believes it will meet the individual or organization's needs related to their interfaces. Personality will vary to meet the different environments that the individual or organization presently encounters in the day-to-day activities. Rapid changes in behavioral patterns usually indicate a change in personality, not in culture.

We always worry about the individual who makes a 180° change in his or her operating mode overnight, even if the change is in the direction that builds more resiliency. Anybody who can change overnight can easily change back again to the original behavior patterns. We would much rather see an individual who moves ahead in thinking and slips back three steps and then moves ahead four steps only to slip back two steps, and so on. This is the type of individual whose personality is changing; in any organization, the personality of the organization has to change before the culture changes within the organization. Going up the ladder one rung at a time is much more effective than trying to jump from the ground to the roof.

CULTURE CHANGE MANAGEMENT

If you are like me when I get a new book, I skim through it until I get to something unique, different, or in direct line with a current project. I then study that part of the book very carefully. Well, you are at that part in this text.

Adoption of a total quality management, supply chain management, CRM, or most other philosophy will have some cultural implications. For some organizations, it may be a minor cultural modification, but for many, the adoption of a new philosophy requires a major cultural shift. In any case, the current culture is a huge issue that must be addressed for change projects and new product to be implemented, successfully. Because culture is difficult to understand, to measure, and to manage, it is relatively easy to ignore. Commonly, organizations ignore it or do not treat corporate culture as a key variable when implementing a major change initiative. Obviously, the "best practice" is just the opposite. Senior management must understand the strategic importance of the overall culture to the change initiative and work hard to understand and manage the impact that culture has on the successful implementation of improvement projects and new products.

Personality is defined as the way an individual or group reacts to a specific set of circumstances. An individual's personality will undergo major shifts during a single day based on specific conditions the individual finds himself or herself in at that particular point in the day. A young man may be very shy and bashful when he's talking to a girl who is his age, but put him out on a football field and he could immediately become very aggressive and unforgiving. There is a great difference in my personality from when I am talking with our minister and when I am talking with my friends as we play cards. In organizations, it is relatively easy to change an organization's personality, but it is very difficult to change the organization's beliefs and habits. If you tell an employee he will be fired if he comes in late one more time, his personality will frequently change, and he will be very prompt. This usually lasts for a short period of time when the culture rejects the personality changes and the employee falls back into the same old habits. For example, when a new manager is assigned to an area, the personality of the area will change to reflect that individual's expectations and priorities. Later on, when the new manager is replaced, the area undergoes another personality change to be in line with the expectations and priorities of the second manager. This does not mean that the culture (beliefs and habits) of the area has changed. For example, I have been a chief executive officer (CEO) of a number of organizations. At one particular organization when I took over as CEO, the organization was just about 6 months away from declaring bankruptcy. Another organization that I was CEO of had a good positive revenue stream, and every indication was that it would continue to grow rapidly. In each of these cases, it was necessary for me to have very different personalities, but my beliefs and habits did not change. To put it another way, personality is short-term behavior, and culture is long-term habits and beliefs.

Organizational culture is the basic pattern of shared beliefs, behaviors, norms, values, and expectations acquired over a long period of time by members of an organization. Organizational personalities reflect the way the present management team is operating. If an improvement project or a change initiative of any kind is consistent with that set of behaviors, beliefs, norms, values, and expectations, then the organization's personality and culture are actually enablers or facilitators of that change. But a change project may be fundamentally counter to the organization's personality and culture, making acceptance of the change much more difficult.

Whenever there is a discrepancy between change in culture and existing culture, existing culture wins. So, to apply this "best practice" to any change initiative, we need to understand whether organizational personality and culture are enablers or barriers to the change. If they are barriers, we must identify why they are barriers, what the existing barriers are, and proactively modify the change or modify the organization's personality, or some combination of both, for change objectives to be successfully met. There are only three options available:

- Option 1: Modify the change to be more consistent with the organization's personality and culture.
- Option 2: Modify or change the organization's personality to be more consistent with the achievement of the change objectives.
- Option 3: Ignore options 1 and 2 and plan the change initiative to take significantly longer and cost significantly more than what you may have originally budgeted.

BASIC CCM OPERATING MODE

The basic operating mode of CCM is to involve everyone in the organization in a continuous flow of change opportunities, many of which are self-originated and implemented. It is like any other activity we are involved in—the more we practice and use it, the more comfortable we feel with it. Of course, we still have to handle the project change management activities in parallel with the CCM activities. When possible, we keep the cultural change activities customized to the individual parts of the organization (e.g., retention programs are effective in a manufacturing part of the organization, and patent awards are more effective in research and development). In developing a CCM organization, there is a strong need for sound management principles that are effectively used. A successful CCM organization functions on sound management principles, which include the following typical ethics/practices:

- Aligned organization
- Job security
- Trust in management
- Recognition of good in bad performance
- Participative employee involvement
- Encouragement for risk-taking
- Empowerment
- Teamwork
- Effective rewards and recognition system
- Strong set of basic beliefs that is practiced

- Good balance between cost, production, and quality
- Effective set of performance standards
- Effective five-way communications
- Employee thought of as an investment not a cost

DESIGNING THE CCM PROJECT

Change management is a methodology developed to minimize the risk of not accomplishing the desired result defined by the project or another improvement activity. There are three general classifications of activities that change management is designed to support:

1. Operational changes—These are changes that are designed to focus on the processes that are used to control or manage your organization.
2. Organizational changes—These are changes that impact the organization chart and the roles and responsibilities within units in your organization.
3. Product improvement/development—These are changes that impact the product or service output that you are providing to your external customer.

These are all changes that PCM was designed to handle one at a time. By definition, projects all have a fixed start and end time limit. (For example, the first ship date of the new product will be January 16, 2019.) But culture change requires the adoption of a different behavioral pattern that requires careful nurturing in order to sustain the culture. (For example, in order to meet the January 16, 2019, new product ship date, it was an executive decision to skip the final testing for the first two weeks of production and have resources available to support the product if there was a problem. The culture and principles of the organization on this matter were, "all of our products are subjected to a thorough evaluation prior to shipping them to external customers." This was purely a risk decision where an immediate situation took precedence over culture and principles.)

If you want to make a change in the organization's culture, it should be done in a very formal, structured way. To accomplish this, we treat the CCM activity as 1- to 3-year improvement activities with the following mission statement: "Develop and implement a strategy that will change the organization's culture so that it encourages and requires every employee to be more creative and innovative." We chose to emphasize creativity and innovation as two separate items, because frequently there are parts of the organization and changes to the organization that are creative but not innovative. (For example, a new organizational structure could be very creative but does not meet the requirements to be considered innovative.) Many of the continuous improvement activities depend on the individuals being creative, as they often make minor changes to the present processes. Most of the Six Sigma projects require creativity, but these are not considered innovative projects. A promotional plan prepared by marketing is often very creative but seldom considered as innovative. Innovative ideas usually take on the project management format, where the creativity initiatives are usually handled as part of the normal job assignment. To change the culture, we are looking at activities that are repeated so often they become a habit rather than a special project, and as a result they are seldom considered innovative.

For an activity to be considered innovative, it must be

- A new and unique idea
- Something that the external customer considers value-added
- Something that is made available to the external customer

For an activity to be considered creative, it must be

- A new and unique idea

As you can see, for anything to be innovative, it must also be creative.

THINKING OUTSIDE OF THE BOX

We hear a lot of discussion about getting the benefits by looking "outside of the box," but unfortunately, many often misinterpret it and do not understand the needs of their customers and the other boxes that are in close proximity. Basically, this is a good thought pattern, but it has one major flaw. There are many boxes within the organization. Some of these are stagnant, while others are going through drastic change (see Figure 14.1). The boxes that are in the transformation state begin to feel

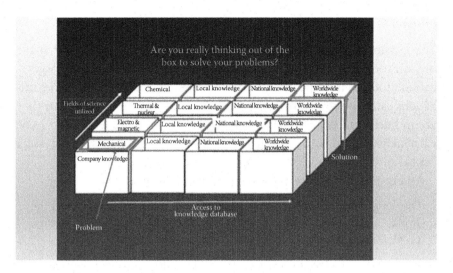

FIGURE 14.1
The many boxes in an organization.

that the organization is in a stagnant state, because management seems to believe that there is no reason for change. For this reason, we need to have an excellent ICM communication system that highlights the positive changes that are taking place in all of the boxes that make up the organization. You would be surprised at how many times someone in a remote box has the best possible answer for a problem or opportunity.

ICM METHODOLOGY IMPLEMENTATION

Phase 1: Cultural/Project Assessment

It is imperative that you understand the organization's culture in order to optimize performance.

Phase 2: Include Change Management in the Organization's Vision, Values, and Objectives

If you don't know where you're going, it's only luck if you get there.

H. J. Harrington

Mission Statement

The mission statement is essential, because it explains the role that the organization was created to fulfill. It is absolutely essential that an organization's future vision be in line with the mission statement. Some organizations call this their "purpose statement" or the "central reason why they are in business." A good mission statement will require leadership to be extremely focused with customers in mind and will serve as a motivating "to be" or "to do."

An example of a "to be" mission for Boeing is the following:

> Our long-range mission is to be the number 1 aerospace company in the world, and among the premier industrial firms, as measured by quality, profitability, and growth.

An example of a "to do" mission for McDonald's is the following:

> To satisfy the world's appetite for good foods, well served, and at a price people can afford.

Winners make their mission statements short, clear, and compelling; losers have missions focused on stakeholder values or some other noncustomer, noncompetitive emphasis. The emphasis on being a leader is essential to both developing the strategy and motivating the organization's people, customers, and suppliers by focusing on being a winner, not a follower.

Values

Values can be defined as the deeply ingrained operating rules or guiding principles of an organization. Some may see them as the specific cultural attributes that drive behavior. The winning organizations set out to create a specific culture and operating style to further define their strategic change and focus.

Unlike mission statements, which are primarily for internal consumption, value statements cannot be inspirational; they must be realistic. For example, Merck's value statement is brief and powerful: "To preserve and improve human life." Another example is that Owens Corning Fiberglas uses "guiding principles" in place of "values." Their guiding principles are as follows:

- Customers are the focus of everything we do.
- People are the source of our competitive strength.
- Involvement and teamwork is our method of operation.
- Continuous improvement is essential to our success.

- Open, two-way communication is essential to the improvement process and our mission.
- Suppliers are team members.
- Profitability is the ultimate measure of our efficiency in serving our customer's needs.

Call them basic beliefs, guiding principles, or operating rules. Call them what you will. The important thing is that they must be defined, and the organization must live up to them, for they surely are the "Stakeholders' Bill of Rights."

In contrast, losing organizations tend not to have explicit values, or they have "hollow" values, or perfectly stated values that no one operates by.

Strategic Focus

Organizations that have been successful in part due to good planning know that they must provide their employees with a road map to help translate the vision and mission into "things people can do."

The next most critical element of what is in a good business plan is the strategic focus of the organization in terms of "how" the vision will compete. The key factors where organizations need to compete are defined as follows:

- **Core competencies**—The technologies and production skills that underlie an organization's products or services (e.g., Sony's skill at miniaturization).
- **Core capabilities**—The business processes that visibly provide value to the customer (e.g., Honda's dealer management processes).
- **Strategic excellence positions**—Unique and distinctive capabilities that are valued by the customer and provide a basis for competitive advantage (e.g., Avon's distribution system).

These leading definitions are actually quite compatible, and a debate over which is proper is not time well spent for most organizations. Regardless of the definitions applied, what is common among all the successful organizations is their ability to identify those four or five key areas of strategic focus that are characterized by the following:

- Customers value the benefits that the focus provides.
- Concentration of resources toward being the absolute best in your chosen areas of emphasis will enable you to excel.

- Excellence in these areas will be difficult for competitors to imitate.
- These areas of focus are your organization's capabilities or what you are really good at, not outcome measures like market share, profit margin, and so on.

The clarity provided by having a few key goals to focus on can help set the foundation for dramatic improvements in business results. For example, years ago, Hewlett-Packard established the lowering of their product failure rate as one of their key business goals. They also coupled this goal with a very clear objective or measurement, with the specific target being a tenfold improvement in results. Their continuing success in a number of rapidly changing markets speaks for itself.

Critical Success Factors—Obstacles to Success

Planning with a leadership emphasis requires a focus much beyond where you are today. Pushing your vision into the future often requires "thinking out of the box" or an unconstrained strategic perspective. The winning planning processes link this back into today's reality, by specifically focusing on the obstacles to success or things that would prevent implementation of the plan. These obstacles can range from the lack of sufficient funding to excessive organizational layers. The point here is to better link the vision to today's starting reality, and be honest enough to highlight and correct the obstacles. This often creates several additional strategies to be incorporated into the plan. Winning organizations will attack this with a positive attitude, while losers will use it to tell themselves they cannot do anything about it. Many organizations will translate the obstacles to success (things in your control that prevent you from successfully implementing the plan) into critical success factors (things that you must do right in order to succeed). This positive transition can help set the proper winning tone on the challenges of moving forward.

Establishing Expectations (Measurements)

One of the major purposes of a business plan is to define what management and the stockholders expect from the organization's performance over the next 5–10 years and then to communicate how success will be measured. The outputs that are used to communicate these expectations are as follows:

- Business objectives—These are used to define what the organization wishes to accomplish over the next 5–10 years.

    Example: IBM released the following objectives that it planned to accomplish during a 10-year period:
    - To grow with the industry.
    - To exhibit product leadership across our entire product line. To excel in technology, value, and quality.
    - To be the most effective in everything we do. To be the low-cost producer, the low-cost seller, the low-cost administrator.
    - To sustain our profitability, which funds our growth.
- Performance goals—These are used to quantify the results that will be obtained if the business objectives are satisfactorily met.

How often have you heard the saying, "Anything worth having is worth working for!"? So it goes with business or strategic planning, but how can we tell if our efforts are paying off? We can surely see sales, profits, and cash flow, all tangible measures of current business results. Both winners and losers utilize these very traditional measures. However, the winners tend to also track some very simple measures or objectives related to their progress in developing long-term competitive strength in their chosen areas of strategic focus. For example, if unsurpassed service is one of the areas of strategic focus, the management of the winners would have regular reporting on a few simple measures of unsurpassed service. These measures might even include things like the number of customer referrals, in addition to measures like customer problem resolution cycle times and the customer retention rate. This linking of very visible, regularly communicated measures to the strategic focus of the organization is crucial to the transition process required to make that vision become a reality. Losers tend to rely only on traditional financial measures to gauge their success.

Another reason why selecting and defining measures is important is their value in informing the organization of the pace of change and implementation required. Organizations that expect quantum leaps in performance against measures will need to prioritize and focus their resources in support of these stretch targets. Winners exhibit a keen flexibility and an intuitive sense of how far to stretch, and seldom set the easy-to-beat or absolutely unrealistic targets that losers tend to use. As we saw with Hewlett-Packard when John Young set aggressive targets (e.g., 10 times improvement in a critical business process within 10 years), they will use this to substantially reprioritize their resources and to create a compelling challenge for their organization to rally around.

Business Objectives

Business objectives set the direction for the organization over a period of time. They are a well-publicized set of objectives that provide management and the employees with information related to what the organization wants to accomplish in the next 5–10 years. These should be very aggressive and should set challenges for the total organization. No one feels good about reaching an easy objective, but we all feel great when we accomplish something that even we thought was out of our reach. As an example, Motorola set "stretch" objectives for itself. William J. Weisz, chief operating officer of Motorola, explained, "We have developed as one of our top 10 goals of the company, the defined 5-year, Tenfold Improvement Program. This means that no matter what operation you are in, no matter what your present level of quality performance, whether you are a service organization or manufacturing area, it is our goal to have you improve that level by an order of magnitude in 5 years." The result of these aggressive objectives has increased Motorola's market in Japan and in the United States and resulted in them winning the Malcolm Baldrige National Quality Award. The president of the organization was once told by one of his vice presidents that there was no way they could improve 10 times in just 5 years of doing business as they were; they might be able to reach 10%–20% per year, but not 200% per year. The president answered, "You are right. You cannot improve that much doing business as you are. You've got the message."

Performance Goals

Performance goals can take the form of short- and long-range targets that support the business objectives. They should be quantifiable, measurable, and time related (e.g., increase sales at a minimum rate of X% per year from 2018 to 2023, with an average annual growth rate of Y%). A typical long-range performance goal would be to decrease the cost of maintaining customer-purchased equipment at a minimum rate of 10% per year for the next 5 years; or to correct 99.7% of all customer problems with one service call per customer over the next 24 months. Each year, a set of short-range goals should be generated by first-line and middle management, directly tied into their budgets. These goals should be reviewed and approved by top management to be sure they support the business objectives and are aggressive enough.

Note: Goals have two key ingredients. First, they specifically state the target for improvement; second, they give the time interval in which the improvement will be accomplished.

> The nice thing about not having a clear vision of where you want to go. You don't have any trouble getting there.

> **H. J. Harrington**

Phase 3: Develop a CCM Plan

This is a very different plan than the performance improvement plan as it focuses on changing behavior patterns rather than producing products. When we are talking about changing culture, it is more effective to make a gradual change than a rapid change. People who make a 180° turn overnight likely will revert back to the old habit patterns soon thereafter.

Definition:

- **Habits** are protectable behavior patterns that have been repeated over and over again until they happen automatically without thought or preplanning. Habits are formed over a long period of time for a series of favorable results as viewed from the individual's standpoint that occurred as a result of an action he or she has taken. Developing favorable habits is one of the primary objectives of the CCM methodology.
- **Cultural assessments** are the primary drivers that help define the cultural improvement tools, which are the ones that should be included in your CCM plan. The three assessments that were conducted in Phase I provide a good road map for a team made up of executives, union officers, and employees. These should be used to construct the CCM plan and to gain buy-in for the plan from the various levels within the organization.

The following activities make up a typical CCM plan:

- Activity 1. Form a team, prepare the project's future state objectives/vision statement, and get it approved.
- Activity 2. Conduct an assessment to determine AS/IS status.
- Activity 3. Develop a future-state targeted operational document.
- Activity 4. Ensure organizational alignment.

- Activity 5. Develop a CCM change approach plan.
- Activity 6. Develop a value proposition and get it approved and funded.
- Activity 7. Develop the CCM project plan.
- Activity 8. Prepare a detailed 6-month plan of action that is included in the CCM project files.
- Activity 9. Get the business case approved and the project included in the organization's active project portfolio.
- Activity 10. Define behavioral patterns that could be used to indicate how culture, innovation, and creativity are changing.
- Activity 11. Implement the detailed 6-month plan, and evaluate results.
- Activity 12. Prepare a detailed 7–18 months plan of action that is included in the CCM project files.
- Activity 13. Implement the 7–18 months plan, and evaluate results.
- Activity 14. Prepare a detailed 19–36 months *Measurement and Reinforcement Plan* of action that is included in the CCM project files.
- Activity 15. Implement the 19–36 months *Measurement and Reinforcement Plan*, and evaluate results.
- Activity 16. Maintain the *Measurement and Reinforcement Plan* from Activity 15 to ensure the cultural change is not superficial.

In analyzing these 16 innovation activities, we find that they apply to change activities in all **five** of the following *major innovation areas*:

1. Management
2. Products
3. Processes
4. Marketing and sales
5. Support services

To change the organization's culture, there needs to be a change in behavior and habits of these five major innovation areas. To accomplish this, we suggest using the following 10 organization cultural drivers, which consists of McKinsey's 7Ss plus three additional ones, including the following:

1. Shared vision—Review and update if necessary the organization's purpose and principles.

2. Strategies—Define the approach that will be used to bring about the desired cultural change.
3. Structure—Organize the way the impacted areas are restructured to support the proposed cultural change.
4. Staffing—Define the criteria for the affected areas.
5. Systems—The efficiency and effectiveness of the critical business processes.
6. Specialized technology/information technology systems—The effective use of information technology to handle the boring repetitive jobs and increase value-added per employee.
7. Systematic change management—How to minimize resistance to the cultural change and prepare the organization for future changes.
8. Skills—The individual's education and life experiences develop skills within the individual that are critical for their quality of work life and their existence. How do you select the right skills for the particular job assignments in the impacted areas?
9. Style/personality—This is the impression that a person leaves after he or she comes in contact with someone. Most people have many different personalities based on their environment and the individuals involved. It is the style that makes up an individual work area based on how the individuals interface with each other. The managerial style usually has the biggest impact on the impacted area.
10. Situation knowledge management—The way knowledge is generated, captured, documented, and communicated throughout the organization. Knowledge is a mixture of experience, practices, traditions, values, contextual information, expert insight, and interpretation that provides an environment and framework for evaluating and incorporating new experiences and information. It is divided into two major categories: explicit and tacit. Knowledge management is a strategy that turns an organization's intellectual assets, both recorded information and the talents of its members, into greater productivity, new values, and increased competitiveness.

It is easy to see how these 10 *cultural drivers* have a major impact on the area's behavior and habits.

15

Culture Change Management Process

THE CULTURE CHANGE MANAGEMENT PLAN

Most major cultural change initiatives (innovative change management [ICM]) are a combination of culture change management (CCM) and project change management (PCM). PCM ensures that the individual projects are in line with the desired cultural change, and CCM drives a change transformation across the organization that is in line with the organization's mission, goals, and objectives. The CCM plan is a combination of the CCM and PCM initiatives. The following are the detailed activities that make up a typical innovative CCM initiative.

Activity 1. Form a Team, Prepare the Project's Future State Objectives/Vision Statement, and Get It Approved

The executive management team should appoint a group of highly creative individuals who represent a cross section of the organization to develop and assist in the implementation of a CCM initiative. If the organization is a union shop, be sure you have a credible representative of the union as a member on this team. There should be at least one member on this team who represents the board of directors. An executive sponsor should also be assigned. This person often is the chief executive officer or president of the organization who also serves as the initiating sponsor.

At the first meeting of the CCM team, the initiating sponsor should explain why the team was formed and indicate the level of change that is desired. To ensure there is no misunderstanding related to the assignment, the CCM team will prepare a future state vision statement that is submitted to the executive committee for approval.

A typical CCM team future state vision statement could read as follows:

Our objective is to change both the hard (explicit) and soft (tacit) parts of the Mignosa Data Analysis LTD culture so that failed project rates are decreased by 40%–50%. And 40% of our annual revenue will be generated by products that were not available 5 years before. Every 3 months all employees will submit at least one self-generated ideal that is implemented.

Activity 2. Conduct an Assessment to Determine AS/IS Status

Management is responsible for determining how the resources within the organization will be utilized. Getting a proper picture of the AS/IS situation is absolutely critical to make meaningful decisions. Management should be sure that the information it is using to make a decision reflects the reality as seen by the executive team, board of directors, middle management, line management, employees, and current and potential customers. It must be sure that the assessment covers the proper considerations and that the data that the assessment team present are accurate as reported. We recommend that at least one executive be assigned to participate physically in the assessment so that he or she has a practical view of the AS/IS status. This provides this executive with the background so that he or she can attest to the assessment's accuracy.

Five types of assessments should be made at this point in the process. The five types of assessments were discussed in Section III.

They are as follows:

- Assessment 1. Innovation maturity analysis
- Assessment 2. Change history analysis
- Assessment 3. Employee opinion survey
- Assessment 4. Customer focus groups
- Assessment 5. Is/should be analysis

Activity 3. Develop a Future-State Targeted Operational Document

By this point in the process, you should have an excellent understanding of the AS/IS conditions within your organization. Now is the time to determine what you want to change and how big a change you want to make. Some consultants call this the organization's "vision statement." We believe it should be all that plus more. We personally do not like open-ended vision statements. We believe that each of these future-state operational documents should have a measurable goal and time interval associated with it. A typical example would be: "By June 1, 2022 (48 months from now), the culture within Mignosa Data Analysis LTD will change to the point that creativity and innovation will be managed at the same priority levels as profit and customer satisfaction. This will largely be accomplished by changing the management system resulting in higher levels of employee and customer satisfaction. The project will include establishing a measurement system that will validate both the hard (explicit data) and soft (tacit data) parts of the new culture. Forty percent of our annual revenue is being generated by products that were not available 5 years before, and 80% of our employees will be suggesting a minimum of four ways to improve the organization's efficiency and/or effectiveness that are implemented each year." (Note: We believe that increasing the creativity of individual thinking will greatly increase the number of innovative ideas considered by the organization.)

Activity 4. Ensure Organizational Alignment

The organization's interfaces, bureaucracy, and communication systems play a big role in determining how to introduce CCM into the organization. Clearly defined mission statements should be developed for all natural work teams. Conflict and responsibilities between natural work teams need to be resolved in order to keep the CCM initiative on schedule. The alignment has to be both vertical and horizontal within the department.

Activity 5. Develop a CCM Change Approach Plan

There are two very different ways to go about developing your CCM change approach:

- The cookie-cutter approach
  This approach is usually recommended by books and consultants. Often this approach is based on one or two projects that the author or consultant has been involved in. They bring what they believe are best general practices and designs to you and organize your management system around them. Often this approach is met by some success, but often it ends in complete failure as a result of misapplying the CCM methodology. The advantage to this approach is that it

requires less executive involvement. If it is successful, everyone can take credit for the job well done. But if it fails, no one is to blame except the methodology. We see this all of the time with projects like Six Sigma. Two organizations use the same training background and the same implementation approach. For one organization, the results are successful; yet, the other organization has very little success with the Six Sigma installation because they did not get the desired results. Let me assure you it is not the methodology that is at fault; it is how it was implemented.

• The customized approach

This approach relies heavily on the data collected during the assessment to determine which tools and methodologies will provide the best results for your organization. We call this the "Thanksgiving" approach. Instead of trying to load our plates up with everything at one time, we start off by just putting some of the mashed potatoes on the plate. A little later we add the turkey. Everything goes on the plate just as it is needed, eliminating much of the waste that goes down the disposal when we take everything at once. We prefer taking the conservative approach where every 3–6 months an improvement tool is added to your toolbox and sufficient time has elapsed so that your employees become skilled with this new tool before the next tool is introduced. This approach also allows the executive team to evaluate how much CCM is value added for the organization after a short period of time and minimum additional resources invested. It also allows your employees to gain skills in handling ongoing changes, resulting in a low-level stress related to their implementation as they know well in advance what is coming. This becomes the point in your organization where people start to look forward to change rather than resist change. Now when Christmas comes around, the results of our Thanksgiving dinner have been digested, and your organization is ready to celebrate and give out gifts.

Activity 6. Conduct a Value Proposition and Get It Approved and Funded

Definition

Value proposition: A value proposition is a document that provides an early stage estimate of the net benefits that will result from the implementation of a change or the use of an output by one or more of the organization's stakeholders. A value proposition can apply to an entire organization, parts thereof, or customer accounts, or product, or services, or internal processes.

A value proposition is usually prepared by the team that is working on the specific project. It reflects their estimate of the cost to design, implement, and operate a specific change or opportunity. It is an early step in analyzing a proposal to determine if it should be included in the organization's portfolio of active projects. It also includes an estimate of the number of units that will be processed and the price per unit that it will sell for. The key measurement is return on investment. In most organizations, when the value proposition is prepared by the project team, the actual cost to implement it is significantly higher than estimated, and the actual revenue is significantly lower than estimated. The accuracy of the estimates can be as high as ±40% of the nominal value.

The value proposition serves as the chief initial document for projects. It is often used to determine if the project should be terminated or funded up to the business case analysis. It includes all the key efficiency and effectiveness parameters, and often includes the allowable tolerance bands on things like speed, reliability, size, and weight. It is used for innovative and not innovative projects that are proposed for the organization.

Activity 7. Develop the CCM Project Plan

Most CCM projects will have a project plan developed uniquely for them. This will include sections on the following:

- Project integration management
- Project scope management
- Project management
- Project cost management
- Project quality management
- Project human resource management
- Project communication management
- Project risk management
- Project procurement management
- Managing organizational change
- Project information technology management

A key part of the project plan document is a work breakdown structure that explains who will be doing a specific part of the project plan and what inputs are required to do each assigned task. It also includes what outputs are required for each task. This work breakdown structure provides an overall guide to all individuals working on the project. It also defines what outputs are needed, when they must be available, and where the output goes. From the project team's standpoint, the work breakdown structure is the "Holy Grail" for the project. It answers the questions of who, what, when, and where. You should read the book entitled, *Project Change Management*, by Daryl R. Conner, H. James Harrington, and Nicholas L. Horney if you would like more information on how CCM and project management complement each other.

Activity 8. Prepare a Detailed 6-Month Plan of Action That Is Included in the CCM Project Files

This is a breakdown by week and sometimes by day of what each individual on the project is doing and reconfirming that each input will be delivered on schedule. It allows additional resources to be shifted to activities that are running behind schedule with the objective of making up for lost time. In reality, this is a finer breakdown of the work breakdown structure. It also allows projects to have steady interdependencies, thereby maximizing the use of individuals and minimizing lost time.

Activity 9. Get the Business Case Approved and the Project Included in the Organization's Active Project Portfolio

Definition

A **business case** captures the reasoning for initiating any project or program. It is most often presented in a well-structured written document, but, in some cases, also may come in the form of a short verbal agreement or presentation. The logic behind the business case is: whatever resources, such as money or effort that will be consumed by the project/activity, should be in support of a specific business need or opportunity.

The business case will need to have a great deal more backup to justify its estimates related to cost-to-implement, cost-to-maintain, return on investment, validation of the assumptions, impact on other initiatives, skills the people implementing the change need to have, analysis of change resistance, and thoroughness of the potential risk analysis. We like to see the business case developed by an independent team, rather than the project team.

An independent analysis will be more likely to give you unbiased estimates than the project team that is enthusiastic about the individual project.

Activity 10. Define Behavioral Patterns That Could Be Used to Indicate How the Culture, Innovation, and Creativity Are Changing

Cultural change is hard to measure. It is a dimension of the mind, not a physical dimension. It takes a great deal of time to determine if a manager's or employee's activity is based on modifying his or her personality versus when it becomes habit. You are fortunate if you started the project by conducting the analysis using one or more of the five analysis tools. This provides your organization with a starting point that can be used to measure the degree of change. But there also is another way that we believe provides early insight in the changing patterns within your culture. The tone of voice, facial expressions, body positioning, hand movements, and many more physical gestures communicate better than words the beliefs of an individual you are having a discussion with. You should make a list of behavioral patterns that reflect the unvoiced feelings that make up the habits and beliefs that exist within your organization and how they need to change. For example, if the employee is unhappy, his face gets red, his voice gets louder, and he grits his teeth. If your manager is managing in a participative style, he or she will let everyone else give their opinions and suggestions before he or she expresses his or her recommendation. Managers who really care always tell "why," not "how." Managers who will not allow failure to occur are stifling innovation.

The team needs to look carefully at their project objectives mission statement and then select keywords and phrases that will have behavioral patterns associated with them. Respect for the individual was one of the most important IBM cornerstones when they were a great company. For example, starting a meeting late is an indication that there is no respect for the individual.

Activity 11. Implement the Detailed 6-Month Plan and Evaluate Results

We prefer to run a virtual online team meeting scheduled for once a week, in place of the weekly meeting with all the team members attending. For this online meeting, each member of the team will submit one or two paragraphs explaining a problem, if they have any. This approach functions on the assumption that unless the individual requires help, there is no need for reporting activities that are on schedule. (For example, activity 217 is 45% complete. It is on schedule.) This approach has a number of advantages and disadvantages. Some of them are as follows:

Advantages

1. Meetings tend to run faster.
2. Personal conversation time is reduced.
3. A separate conference room is not needed.
4. Travel time is reduced.

Disadvantages

1. Less commitment is required to participate in a conference call.
2. Less personal contact is made.
3. It is hard to control a meeting.
4. The tendency is not to stay for the whole meeting. This creates a void in understanding what is going on.

The project manager's responsibility is to keep all of the activities in harmony or to focus management's attention on any activity that is jeopardizing the chance of the project being completed on time, within costs, and at the required efficiency level. Anytime that an individual misses two consecutive weekly reports, the project manager should escalate the situation to the individual's manager, requiring him or her to explain in writing why the individual missed the reporting schedule. And if the activity is now in jeopardy of not being completed on time, the project manager must find out what the manager plans to do to help get the activity back on schedule.

Some cultures prefer to use the standard "once a week" status update approach to tracking the project's progress. This requires more time devoted to providing updated status than in the virtual online system.

At the end of each month, a formal management review will be conducted. The purpose of this review is to report to the executive team the status of the project and to determine if the project should be dropped or funded for an additional 6 months. The project team should look at different means of assessing progress in measuring the cultural change. The project team needs to complete these measurements/indications prior to the 6-month meeting.

Activity 12. Prepare a Detailed 7–18 Month Plan of Action That Is Included in the CCM in Project Files

Note: This activity is the same as Activity 7 with only one difference—it covers 7–18 months of the project plan.

Activity 13. Implement 7–18 Month Plan and Evaluate Results

Note: This activity is the same as Activity 10 with only one difference—it covers 7–18 months of the project plan.

Activity 14. Prepare a Detailed 19–36 Month Measurement and Reinforcement Plan of Action That Is Included in CCM Project Files

This plan is primarily a measurement and stabilization monitoring activity. It is designed to ensure the cultural gains that were made continue as part of the organization's operating mode. In parts of the organization that have not completed the cultural transformation, the plan will include additional change initiatives to bring it in line with the cultural objectives. It covers *months 19–36* of the project plan.

Activity 15. Implement 19–36 Month Measurement and Reinforcement Plan and Evaluate Results

This change focuses on obtaining legitimate measurement results that can measure the impact the project had on creating an innovative/creative culture within the organization. It will also report what needs to be expanded to the measurement activities so that the cultural change's impact on increased revenue or return on investment is calculated. This may be a major problem, because during the cultural change initiative, many other projects have been completed, most of which have had a significant impact on the organization's performance. It is sometimes not worth the effort to make this analysis to separate out the impact that the various projects had on the organization's performance.

Activity 16. Maintain the Measurement and Reinforcement Plan from Activity 15 to Ensure the Cultural Change Is Not Superficial

CCM PLAN DESIGN

The activities are designed so that every 3 months a new learning module is introduced into the organization. Frequently, the new learning modules for innovation and creativity are followed by a learning module on CCM. This is then followed by an innovation and culture learning module. The process is repeated three or four times a year. The learning modules for innovation and creativity are based on the 75 most frequently used innovation tools and methodology (see list in Appendix B) and the mind expanders (see Appendix C). A detailed description of each of these tools and methodologies with help related to using these tools can be found in the following three books:

- *The Innovation Tools Handbook, Volume 1: Organizational and Operational Tools, Methods, and Techniques that Every Innovator Must Know*
- *The Innovation Tools Handbook, Volume 2: Evolutionary and Improvement Tools that Every Innovator Must Know*
- *The Innovation Tools Handbook, Volume 3: Creative Tools, Methods, and Techniques that Every Innovator Must Know*

CHANGE MANAGEMENT

There are four strategic and four tactical risk areas to address. Each of these represents an area of potential vulnerability—failure to address them can jeopardize the project's ability to survive during turbulence created by distractions and resistance to the project.

Definitions

Strategic Change: Those changes that have a significant impact throughout an organization.
Risk Area: Any class of activity or lack of activity that reduces the probability of successful project implementation. Examples include resistance, change knowledge, project overload, and implementation skills and techniques.

Under strategic change conditions, you should be concerned with four strategic risk areas:

- Strategic Risk Area 1. Resilience
- Strategic Risk Area 2. Change knowledge
- Strategic Risk Area 3. Managing adaptation resources
- Strategic Risk Area 4. Understanding important leverage point

Under tactical change conditions, you should be concerned with four strategic risk areas:

- Tactical Risk Area 1. Sponsorship
- Tactical Risk Area 2. Culture
- Tactical Risk Area 3. Resistance
- Tactical Risk Area 4. Agent

STRATEGIC CHANGE RISK AREAS

Strategic Risk Area 1. Resilience

In terms of increasing the organization's speed of change to support the implementation of a critical project or a new product, a critical ingredient for you to consider is the degree to which key people on the project team and those impacted by the project are resilient. The speed of change and resiliency are directly related. The more resilient your organization employees are, the greater is its speed of change. There are seven supporting patterns for resiliency: nature, process, roles, resistance, commitment, culture, and synergy.

Strategic Risk Area 2. Change Knowledge

Change knowledge is management's and the team's working knowledge of change concepts. This includes the in-depth understanding of how the change unfolds within an organization and among individuals.

Strategic Risk Area 3. Managing Adaptation Resources

Managing adaptation resources is the degree to which change decisions take into account the efficient utilization of typically scarce allocation (adaptation) resources. This includes the alignment of an organization's changes, goals, plans, visions, and organizational structure, with the resources available for implementing the change.

Strategic Risk Area 4. Understanding Important Leverage Points

It is important to understand important leverage points in the implementation process and make effective use of them to make critical no-go decisions and to gain additional management commitment to the project.

TACTICAL CHANGE AREAS

- Tactical Risk Area 1. Sponsorship—Failure to have the initiating and sustaining sponsors to appropriately sanction the change frequently will cause a project to fail. It requires building and sustaining commitment from those in a position to sponsor the project.
- Tactical Risk Area 2. Culture—The introduction of a change that is inconsistent with the existing culture represents a major problem and major delays. You must have alignment between the culture and the project objectives. If you do not have alignment, you have three possible results:
  1. You can change the project to get alignment.
  2. You can change the culture to be in line with the project.
  3. You can prepare for failure.
- Tactical Risk Area 3. Resistance—This is the lack of understanding of how change unfolds within an organization and among individuals. The inevitable resistance of those who will be expected to change behaviors as a result of the project must be managed.
- Tactical Risk Area 4. Agent—You need to have change agents who know how to diagnose transition problems, build implementation architecture, and assist others in the change process. The problem becomes the lack of having change agents who have been prepared to use the change management skills effectively.

Resiliency operates under the approach, "a trip around the world begins with the first step, then another, and another and you are on your way to your destination."

16

Culture Change Management Tools and Methodologies

PLANNING FOR CULTURE CHANGE MANAGEMENT

Definition

Assimilation stress: The stress put on an individual or organization whenever a change is made, either negative or positive. It is the stress that is required to overcome the status quo. At any one point in time, the total assimilation stress is the accumulated stress of all of the individual assimilation stresses. The stress factor you experience is a combination of personal stress (divorce, moving, having a baby, etc.) plus the stress as related to the work environment and potential new projects.
Future shock: The point at which people can no longer assimilate change without displaying dysfunctional behaviors.

Culture change management (CCM) is based on a very different approach to the one we have been using in project change management (PCM). In PCM, we are very concerned about overloading the workforce with too many changes at the same time driving them into future shock that causes the individual to become dysfunctional. In CCM methodology, for the same complexity of a change initiative over time, there is a continuous reduction in the amount of the assimilation effort required to install the change initiative. In Figure 16.1, we kept the complexity of the change initiatives constant over a 4-year period. The second line represents the number of assimilation points required to absorb that level of change into the organization. Note that the second line continues to decrease in the amount of effort required to install projects of equal complexity.

The real difference between PCM and CCM is the impact it has on the people required to change. With PCM about 10% of the organization's

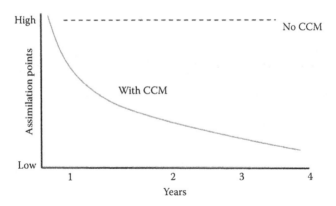

FIGURE 16.1
CCM impact on total assimilation points per average change.

employees are candidates to be part of the PCM methodology each year. They are involved in the methodology for 2–3 months and then never have a chance to practice it again for 3–5 years. This means that on the average, each time a target goes through a PCM process, he or she will not have an opportunity to use it again for an average of 3 years. Over that time period, the affected individuals have settled back into their old culture.

While the objective of the PCM is to assist the project manager in getting the project completed on time and within cost, the objective of the CCM is to provide ongoing opportunities for the individual to adjust to a moderate level of change stress on a regular basis. This approach trains all of the employees to accept and absorb an increasing stress level part of the AS/IS environment through an ongoing series of change opportunities. This approach is based on the belief that the more frequently you do something, the more apt it is to become a personal habit.

START THE CCM METHODOLOGY WITH A NO-LAYOFF POLICY

As you start your CCM methodology, the first thing you need to do is set up a system to protect the individuals on whom you are building the organization's future. The following is a typical no-layoff policy:

A policy that declares that no individual will be laid off because of a performance improvement initiative until all other options have been exhausted.

This does not mean that it may not be necessary to lay individuals off as a result of negative business trends. Under this policy, individuals whose jobs are eliminated are retrained for an equal or more responsible job.

Employee security is one of the most critical and complex political and economic issues facing top management today. Management must determine the following:

- Are the employees an investment or a cost?
- How much improved performance and flexibility would be gained if the organization provided employee security?

Resiliency

Change is not something that just happens. The CEO and his or her key people have to make the case for change and innovation and they have to create an environment that fosters it.

Charles Kalmbach
Managing Partner, Accenture

One key to survival in today's rapidly changing environment is to develop a resilient organization. Resiliency is not invented, it is liberated.

Definition

Resiliency: The ability to absorb high levels of disruptive change while displaying minimum dysfunctional behavior.

In order to increase an organization's ability to absorb change, the resiliency of the project team and those who are impacted by the change (change targets) is an important factor. The more resilient the organization is, the greater its speed of change. A resilient organization has five characteristics:

- Positive attitude: Displaying a sense of security and self-assurance that is based on their view of life as complex but filled with opportunity
- Focused attitude: Having a clear vision of what they want to achieve
- Flexible attitude: Demonstrating a special pliability in thinking and in working with others when responding to change
- Organized attitude: The ability to develop and find order in ambiguity
- Proactive attitude: Engaging change rather than defending against it

We liken the resilient person to a capacitor and the resistant person to a resistor. In an electronic circuit, the resistor just sets there burning up energy, but the capacitor stores up energy so that it can be used when needed.

The resilient person can increase his or her future shock level up to 1500 assimilation points and at the same time reduce the peak assimilation of the individual changes by as much as 50% while reducing the change impact duration by as much as 25%. This provides the organization with a very competitive advantage.

Resiliency is not a tool or a methodology; it is an attitude, a culture, the way we behave, and our beliefs. No organization can transform itself into a resilient organization overnight. It takes time to bring about the transformation. When an individual's original level of resiliency is raised through training, coaching, and rewards, it is referred to as "raising baseline resiliency to an enhanced level." As the individuals who make up the organization base resilience level move up to the enhanced level, the organization's cultures and behaviors will change to reflect this new level of resiliency.

Organizations can measure the resiliency enhancement level by monitoring the organization's changes in behavior as defined by the five resilient characteristics. It is our experience that when a group of resilient people are impacted by change, a great deal of synergy occurs.

Resilient employees live with the same change challenges that everyone else has, but they usually possess the following traits:

- They are physically and emotionally healthier.
- They rebound from the change faster and with less stress.
- They achieve more of the objectives.
- They are more productive.
- They have a higher level of implementation capacity.
- They develop a resilient culture.

Winners look at change as building blocks. Those that fight change, find themselves as the foundation that someone else builds upon.

H. J. Harrington

A common source of implementation failure is low personal or team resilience. Resilient people and teams "bounce back" from major changes stronger and more capable than before. Organizational Development Resources (ODR) has used the *Personal Resilience Questionnaire* in their research. This tool is designed to measure an individual's level of the specific characteristics that are linked to resilience. Feedback to individuals is given in the form of the *Personal Resilience Profile*. One aspect of resilience is the amount of energy (mental, physical, and emotional resources) we have available to recalibrate expectations after being disrupted by change. Some of this is determined by physical and psychological makeup (heredity), and some of it is related to the way we treat our bodies (e.g., the food we eat and the activities we choose).

A third but equally important aspect of resilience is the way we use our mental, emotional, and physical resources in our daily lives. We have chosen to focus on how people use and manage their resources as they deal with the disruption of major change.

Five Types of Personal Attitudes

The following characteristics have been identified as personal attributes that enable individual resilience during change:

- Positive attitude: Displaying a sense of security and self-assurance that is based on their view of life as complex but filled with opportunity
- Focused attitude: Having a clear vision of what they want to achieve
- Flexible attitude: Demonstrating a special pliability in thinking and in working with others when responding to change
- Organized attitude: The ability to develop and find order in ambiguity
- Proactive attitude: Engaging change rather than defending against it

Positive Attitude

There are two aspects to this characteristic: world and yourself. Let's look at "world" first. Most situations, and most people, have both positive and negative aspects to them. Research shows that people differ in their tendency to focus on the positive or the negative elements. Those who tend to focus on the positive, view their environment (i.e., the world) as complex and challenging. They are able to see opportunities and possibilities in situations that at first may look like problems. Those who focus primarily on the negative can get into cycles of anxiety and depression that prevent them from seeing value and opportunity in circumstances. Having a basically optimistic outlook is important, since it allows one to find ways to turn negative situations around. In addition, people who have a positive attitude toward their environment are better able to create situations that are positive.

- Key Indicators
  - Is generally upbeat about the future
  - Finds opportunities in times of turmoil
  - Looks for the good in what appear to be bad situations

Positive "yourself" refers to a belief in oneself as a valuable, capable person, and this can be extremely powerful. People need a strong foundation from which to face uncertainty and stress in the world. This foundation can be developed through realistically assessing one's capabilities and achieving self-acceptance while continuing to learn and grow. When a person feels capable of reaching his or her goals, that person is able to take action confidently and can weather failure without losing the feeling of self-worth. Also related to this positive view of self is the belief that one can influence the environment and what happens in one's life, rather than the belief that external forces operate to determine one's fate. Positive, resilient people display a sense of security and self-assurance that is based on their view of life as complex, but filled with opportunity.

- Key Indicators
  - Have high self-esteem
  - Believe that their actions can influence situations and people
  - Avoid feeling victimized by circumstances
  - Believe in their abilities—"can-do" attitude
  - Look for the good, not the bad
  - Look forward to a better future
  - Have a high level of self-esteem
  - Feel they can influence what is going to happen
  - Are energetic

Focused Attitude

Because change is generally characterized by ambiguity and uncertainty, it should be no surprise that having a strong sense of goals and priorities is important to resilience. Having a sense of purpose and a focus in life is an advantage, because when goals and priorities are clear, it is easier to get back on course following major disruption. Research suggests that people who describe themselves as strongly committed to their goals, or who see their life as having meaning or purpose, are better able to manage confusing situations—to sort out the important issues, judge the relative worth of alternatives, and thus use their personal energy more efficiently. Without a sense of purpose and priorities, resources are likely to be used inefficiently, since every new situation would require a person to predetermine what is important before taking action. Focused people are resilient. They have a clear vision of what they want to achieve. They have demonstrated a special ability in thinking and in working with others when responding to change.

- Key Indicators
  - Have a strong sense of purpose
  - Are able to set goals and prioritize actions
  - Are able to distinguish between critical and trivial objectives
  - Use personal objectives to guide everyday actions and decisions
  - Know what they want
  - Prioritize their efforts based upon impact
  - Align personal and organizational goals
  - Bend with the wind
  - Can adjust to change
  - Can see things from different perspectives
  - Are open-minded
  - Are open to other people's ideas
  - Like to be a member of a team

Flexible Attitude

There are two aspects to this characteristic: thoughts and social. Let's look at "thoughts" first. Coping with the ambiguity that change presents is a critical skill for resilience. An important aspect of this type of coping is the person's ability and willingness to look at situations from multiple points of view, to suspend judgment while considering alternative perspectives, and to accept and live with paradoxes and contradictions as part of life. Many times, when a person is open minded in finding different ways to view a situation, he or she will have a broader understanding of the problem and be able to form more creative, effective resolutions. Flexible thoughts increase the likelihood of finding these creative, effective ways to achieve goals. In contrast, people who would rather have immediate, straightforward solutions may draw conclusions so quickly that they miss information that could be useful.

- Key Indicators
  - Have a high tolerance for ambiguity
  - Are comfortable dealing with paradoxes
  - Have the capacity to see things from different perspectives—open minded
  - Avoid "black or white" thinking

Flexible "social" refers to the ability to draw on the resources of others, adding to one's flexibility. Research indicates that highly resilient people recognize their interdependence with others. They are characterized by strong social bonds that they can rely on for support during difficult times. They are able to form and maintain close relationships, are willing to engage in the "give and take" of mutually supportive friendships, and can recognize ways in which other people's skills can complement their own. If this type of support is either not available or not sought, a person's capacity to deal with stress or uncertainty is decreased.

- Key Indicators
  - Draws on external resources for assistance and support
  - Values the ideas of others
  - Recognizes interdependence
  - Is a good "team player"

Organized Attitude

While flexibility is an asset in allowing one to see the possibilities in situations, another important element of resilience is the ability to organize and to find structure in ambiguity. This feature of resilience enables one to see the order in chaos and move beyond confusion toward action. The discipline required to face complex, convoluted situations, assess the available information, choose a direction in which to proceed, and plan the steps needed to move forward is important. This requires that a person set aside information that may be enticing but is not helpful at the moment, to focus on the elements that are important, and logically structure them into a workable, understandable plan. Without the skill to organize chaotic situations, a person might waste a lot of resources trying one solution, and then another, without making any real progress. Organized people are resilient people who are able to develop and find order in ambiguity.

- Key Indicators
  - Quickly sorts information
  - Builds structure in chaos
  - Plans action for maximum efficient use of resources
  - Avoids acting on impulse
  - Likes structure
  - Groups information effectively
  - Plans their activities

Proactive Attitude

The organization or individual who is proactive initiates action even though the individual is uncertain if the positive or negative nature is an outcome of their actions. To be proactive, one must be willing to take some risks and to endure some discomfort in the belief that positive outcomes (such as growth, personal development, and the achievement of important goals) will result. Proactive individuals seek challenges rather than avoid them and respond to disruption by investing energy in problem solving rather than withdrawing. In contrast, people who place an extremely high value on certainty, stability, and security may pass up valuable opportunities while waiting for a "sure thing" to come along. Proactive resilient people encourage change, rather than defend against it.

- Key Indicators
  - Actively engages change
  - Takes reasonable risks
  - Is willing to try new activities
  - Does not continually strive for predictability and stability
  - Has lots of new ideas
  - Likes to see things moving along
  - Questions the status quo

SPECIALIZED IMPROVEMENT TECHNIQUES AND METHODOLOGIES FOR CCM

What the CCM methodology is looking for is a tune that the fiddler can play and everyone can dance to. Some typical examples are as follows.

Assignment Rotation

This involves moving an employee to another assignment, making the employee more valuable to the organization and providing him or her with additional learning experiences (e.g., research development engineer being reassigned to manufacturing engineering). In some cases, these are temporary assignments for 1 year. This allows the individual whose career path stays within the smokestack environment to not sidetrack his or her career plan. In some organizations, one of the considerations is that employee pay is based on the number of different activities he or she is certified to perform. Basically, when an employee is given a new assignment, the learning opportunity is very high (e.g., 2% more for each new job category). As they gain familiarity with the new assignment, the learning opportunity decreases rapidly. Eventually, it becomes that same old boring assignment. Figure 16.2 is the learning opportunity cycle. At Point A in the cycle, the employee is performing well above standards. At this point in time, the employee can be considered to be rotated to another assignment. Normally, employees are required to work at the new assignment for a minimum of 3 months. To get reassigned, they have increased the performance level to the 8-point scale on the performance evaluation report and have worked on the assignment for a minimum

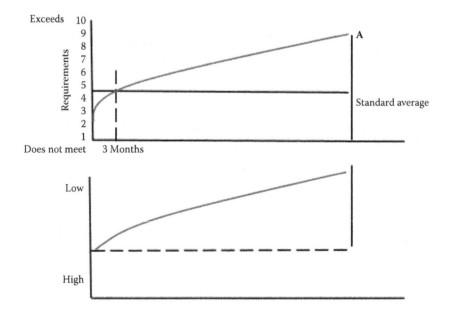

FIGURE 16.2
Learning opportunity curve.

of 3 months. Often these temporary assignments coincide with the employee's career plan. A subassembly operator's long-range goal is to work in human resources. A temporary assignment in human resources provides them with a much better understanding of what the assignment would entail. Career plans are modified based on the employee's knowledge gained during these temporary assignments. The individual's performances during the rotation assignments are evaluated, and as a result they impact the individual's future salary.

Employee Suggestion Program

The suggestion program is primarily directed at nonexempt employees. It provides recognition to the nonexempt employee when he or she has an idea that is implemented within the organization. Many organizations tie in monetary awards related to the value of the suggestion. When I worked for IBM, one of my inspectors received an award worth $1 million in today's money for an idea that he submitted as a suggestion.

The suggestion program is for ideas that are outside of the employee's responsibility. For example, a secretary who suggests the use of a different printer because it would improve productivity; a test operator who suggests redesigning a test fixture so the parts cannot be put in backward; or the repair technician who suggests using a different part because it will last longer in a specific application, and so on. These are all good ideas that will save the organization money and improve its reputation. As a result, the organization should be willing to share the savings from these ideas with the employees who made the suggestions. Usually, the scope of the suggestions requires that someone other than the suggester evaluate and implement the suggestion or at least approve the suggestion before it can be implemented. As a result, these suggestions are submitted into a formal suggestion program.

The key elements of the suggestion program are as follows:

1. The suggestion must not be part of the suggester's responsibility.
2. The suggestion does not have to be implemented to be considered.
3. The suggester shares in the savings resulting from the suggestion.
4. The suggestion cannot be predated by activities or plans already underway.

How does the suggestion process work? The National Cash Register Company developed the concept back in 1896. The value of the suggestion program is that it offers the person closest to the work activity the opportunity to suggest improvements. This results in more effective utilization of assets, increased productivity, waste reduction, lower product costs, and improved quality. As Paul Peterman, then manager of the Field Suggestions at IBM Corporation, put it, "Ideas are the lifeblood of the company, and the suggestions plan is a way of getting these ideas marketed."

The formal suggestion process requires that employees document their ideas for improvement and submit them to a central suggestion department that is responsible for coordinating and evaluating the ideas and reporting back to the employee. The suggestion department reviews each suggestion and chooses an area within the organization that is best suited to evaluate the suggestion. The evaluation area studies the recommended changes to determine if they will provide overall improvement in quality, cost, or productivity. If the suggestion is accepted by the evaluation area, the evaluator will determine what tangible savings will result from implementing the idea.

In some cases, suggestions will be adopted even though the savings are intangible. These ideas benefit the organization, but the savings cannot be measured or estimated in a precise dollar amount. If the idea is rejected, the investigator records the reason why the idea was rejected on the evaluation form. Both the accepted and rejected suggestions are then returned to the suggestion department, where the evaluations are reviewed for completeness and accuracy. A letter is then sent to the employee's manager describing the action that was taken on the suggestion. For an accepted suggestion, a check normally accompanies the letter. Each suggestion is reviewed with the employee by the employee's manager. When major cash awards are received, the manager will usually call a department meeting to present the award to the employee, to publicly recognize the employee, as well as to provide an incentive to get the other members of the department participating in the suggestion program.

Paul Revere Insurance Company employees submitted 20,000 suggestions during the first three years of their improvement process. The suggestions were major contributors to the organization's improved performance:

- Income up 200% with no additional staff
- The organization moved from No. 2 to No. 1 in their field of insurance

Frank K. Sonnenberg, in his article entitled, "It's a Great Idea…But," wrote, "A new idea, like a human being, has a life cycle. It is born. If properly nurtured, it grows. When it matures, it becomes a productive member of society." He points out that at 3M, some people claim that the company's "11th commandment" is, "Thou shalt not kill an idea" (https://www.questia.com/magazine/1G1-12112236/it-s-a-great-idea-but).

Improvement Effectiveness/Good Ideas Program

All individuals and all ideas are eligible for the improvement effectiveness program. Many suggestions are not eligible for the suggestion program. The best approach is to evaluate an idea to see if it is eligible for the suggestion program and if it is not, then turn it in under the improvement effectiveness program after it has been implemented.

Most exempt personnel, due to their positions and job descriptions, are not eligible for the suggestion program. However, they often generate some very good ideas that are implemented, greatly increasing the organization's efficiency and effectiveness. The improvement effectiveness/good ideas program was designed to highlight some of these contributions that are not eligible for the suggestion program. The problem with this approach is that some jobs have a great deal more opportunity to identify improvements of the job assignments. In order to encourage everyone to be creative, the rewards program can be applied to common job descriptions and to individuals who work in the same department.

There are many different approaches used to provide recognition to individuals who create ideas that when implemented increase the organization's efficiency and effectiveness. One approach that is frequently used is to assign points to each improvement idea that the employee comes up with. These points accumulate over time and can be cashed in for merchandise or travel at any time. We know one company's maximum award is tickets for two to fly to Hawaii.

This program is very much like the S&H Green Stamp program that was popular in the 1970s. Another approach that is sometimes offered is to invite the individual with the greatest contribution to have lunch with the chief executive officer.

Creativity Motivation Program

The major focus of many functions within an organization is to solve problems and improve the processes within the organization. These employees get a superior salary compared to the average production worker, so in most cases they are not eligible for the suggestion program. In these areas, we like to make a game of the change process. The engineering functions (research and development, manufacturing, engineering, quality engineering, manufacturing engineering, industrial engineering, etc.) will engage in the process where they compete with other individuals within their function. The recognition is based on the amount of money they save the organization. There is no competition between functions, and the potential for reducing cost varies from function to function.

Definition

Functions: The major parts of the organization that are usually considered as the smokestack of the organization. For example, finance, quality assurance, manufacturing engineering, manufacturing, research and development, human factors, etc.

A list of the functional winners is often accompanied by a description of what they did to win the recognition, which is published in the company's newsletter. In addition, each winner is invited to have lunch with the president of the organization, during which his or her contributions to the organization are discussed, and they receive small plaques or trophies. I know of one organization that gives out lapel pins. Through this program at one IBM plant alone, an additional $260 million savings was recognized in 1 year.

Creativity Enhancement Programs

These are programs that provide creativity training for all employees and set targets for the employees/managers to document a specific number of ideas that are implemented each month. Many companies are now receiving two or more implemented ideas per month per employee, including the president of the organization. Many companies worldwide are using this approach as a means to motivate employees to be more and more creative, and this is in tune with the organization's cultural change activities.

We have seen organizations that are using this type of program as part of their assignment rotation approach. When the number of expected ideas drops below one per month, this signals that the employee is ready to be transferred to another assignment. For example, Dana Corporation asked each employee to submit in writing two ideas a month. Last year, they received 2,000,000 ideas, and over 80% were implemented.

Area Activity Analysis (AAA)

One of the most powerful tools the professional change manager has in his or her toolbox is one called area activity analysis (AAA). This is a tool designed to align an organization's structure and processes. This tool should be used prior to starting your ICM activities. In addition to aligning the organization structure and processes, it also establishes an effective measurement system down to the natural work team levels.

This methodology develops a new individualistic mission part of the organization down to the employee level. It can focus the natural work team that uses the maximum amount of resources. For each of these processes, flowcharting and a measurement system are established. For more information about AAA, we suggest that you read the book, *Area Activity Analysis*, by H. James Harrington, published in 2000.

Management Rotation

One of the best ways to prepare a manager for a future promotion is by giving him or her experience in different management roles. For example, the next step up the ladder for the vice president of sales and marketing would be as president of the organization. The president of the organization needs to have an excellent view of how the total organization functions. By moving a vice president into a different vice president assignment, it will provide this individual with a very different view of the way the organization functions. Individuals who have risen to the executive level should no longer be functional oriented managers but professional managers. Moving a middle-level quality assurance manager over to an assignment as manager of a manufacturing engineering group is an excellent way to determine if the individual has long-range potential in the management ranks. The same type of reasoning applied to first-level managers in all areas being willing to take on a managerial assignment in an area they never worked in indicates that they want to learn how the organization functions. All too often, our managers, who were excellent employees, have no interest in how the organization functions. These usually are excellent engineers who became managers based on their engineering work rather than on their ability to manage people. Assigning excellent engineers to manage groups of people is often harmful to the people they manage and to their potential growth within the organization.

Every time a new manager takes over a group, he or she generates a number of different concepts in order to leave his or her manager's mark on the group. I know of one organization that takes the approach of moving managers into departments they complain about.

Let me give you a personal example. I have been the chief executive officer of a software company, financing company, consulting company, and construction company. Although I spent 20 years in the quality assurance areas of IBM, I do not consider myself a quality assurance manager; I consider myself a professional manager.

Speak-Up Program

Another way to relieve pent-up emotion, identify new opportunities, and provide the employee with answers to the questions is a process called a "speak-up program." This program encourages employees to share with the organization the problems they are having or questions that they may have about the organization that cannot be answered by the immediate managers. Often this involves a problem with their immediate manager that they are reluctant to bring to his attention. Typical examples include sexual harassment, favoritism, unreasonable request, inappropriate activity, and activity not in keeping with the organization's principles. The speak-up program is confidential and never divulges the employee's name. It provides an ombudsman to represent the employee. These speak-up programs allow employees to point out inadequacies in the way they are being managed and to bring about positive change within the organization. Each employee who signs a speak-up request should receive an answer to his or her concern in writing during a confidential meeting.

17

Culture Change Management Summary

The key to successful management is simple: Get back to basics.

- Treating employees as you would like to be treated
- Setting a positive work ethic example
- Encouraging those who fail and praising those who succeed
- Providing honest evaluation of an individual's efforts
- Stepping up to the unpleasant situations
- Being friendly and having a smile on your face
- Portraying a sense of urgency and importance regarding the work that is being performed

As the famous Notre Dame head football coach, Knute Rockne, put it, "The trouble in American life today, in business as well as in sports, is that too many people are afraid of competition. The result is that in some circles people have come to be successful without a great deal of hard work, training, and sacrifice. If you are not willing to give your all to the job, then management is not the right career path for you."

> Team participation should never occur until the management team is participating in the cultural change activities, if you don't want the employee to believe that they are being manipulated. Management must provide visible evidence of the organization's total commitment to a policy of encouraging change, rather than reacting to change.
>
> **H. J. Harrington**

IBM AS AN EXAMPLE OF CULTURAL CHANGE

Unfortunately, our culture in most organizations has changed for the worse over the past 50 years. There has been a deluge of technical reports, consultants' presentations, and books talking about how we need to improve organizational performance and how important mission statements, vision statements, values, goals, and so on are to an organization. The result is primarily a lot of additional paperwork that we depend on someone else implementing. I would much rather have people living up to our values than writing about what they should be. We have too many planners and far too few doers. Let's use my family's careers working for IBM as an example. I worked over 40 years and my wife worked 10 years for IBM. In addition, I have 14 cousins who have worked for IBM, and my father started work at IBM 20 years before I did. He can remember when they hired Thomas Watson, Senior. Some of my very earliest memories with my mother and father were hearing them tell me that they hope that when I grow up, I would get a job at IBM. (I hope my granddaughter will not have to work at IBM.) When I was 3 years old, I had the job of picking up the shells at IBM's pistol range. I started work for IBM when I turned 12 years old setting pins in the bowling alley. (Every Saturday, children from IBM would get together in our own little bowling league. Thomas Watson himself passed out trophies to the winners.) I learned to play golf in IBM's junior golfing league. I was a golf caddy for Thomas Watson, Junior. Every Christmas, IBM held an employees' children's Christmas party with lots of good food and gifts for everyone. When I turned 18, IBM gave me a job in their apprentice program. When I started working full time for IBM, my father and I were given awards and became members of the second-generation club. Think was not a name on the wall; it was how you existed. Anyone who wanted to get ahead took a night class 10 months of the year. As long as you did your job, didn't get drunk, and didn't cause IBM any embarrassment, you had a job for life. For example, when they shut down IBM's activity at Cape Canaveral, they transferred five quality engineers out to California for us to find jobs for them. Within 2 years, all five of them had been transferred back to the East Coast as it was the place that they preferred to live. In each case, IBM picked up the cost of transferring these employees to the West Coast and then transferring them back to the East Coast.

If one of your employees was out sick for 3 days, the manager was expected to visit the employee and volunteer to go to the grocery store or help take your employee to the doctor if he needed it. If one of your employee's immediate family died, the manager was expected to go to the funeral and IBM would send flowers. I remember one case where they sent me overseas to attend the funeral for the mother of an employee who reported to me.

Things have changed at IBM since my retirement in 1985. I recently attended a funeral of an IBM retired manager and no one from IBM was there representing them. IBM used to have an annual dinner and dance for employees who had been with them more than 25 years. Employees really looked forward to this, as it gave us an opportunity to meet some of our old friends. This dinner is a thing of the past.

In the summer, departments used to have departmental picnics to which the entire family was invited. Good food, lots of games, and trophies for the children were distributed.

At that time, IBM was the most admired company in the United States, if not the world. Today, IBM is so far down on the list, it's hard to find. Today, if you ask somebody who works for IBM what he or she does for a living, he or she will usually give you a response like "I am a programmer or other consultant." In the 1950s, if you asked the same question, you would have heard a common response—"I am an IBMer."

In the early twentieth century, IBM managers knew the names of all of their employees' children and what they were planning to do with their lives. Moreover, each employee had a career plan and was trained to think about what job he or she wanted until retirement at age 65. IBM used to be a family organization. Today it's just a place to hang your hat as you look for something better. Employee loyalty has decreased significantly as IBM's commitment to the employee has decreased. Many people blame it on the advancement in technology, but technology has not replaced IBM's commitment to its employees and the employees' commitment to IBM.

Recently, a number of major companies in the United States have stopped allowing employees to work out of a home office in favor of them working out of a main central office.

They are finally beginning to realize that a big part of organizational loyalty occurs at the drinking fountain or in the cubicle next door. You can't help but have a different attitude if a positive person works at the desk beside you than you have about a person you never see or talk to.

The first question that managers need to ask the employee is, "What has changed since our last meeting, and what value was added as a result of the change?"

Do not change for change sake; do it to improve performance.

H. J. Harrington

There are four key ways to make cultural change happen:

1. Communicate the need for change over and over again. The first person to change should be the chief executive officer/president.
2. Leaders need to communicate and demonstrate innovation by their employees with the managers' actions and involvement.

You are not what you say; you are what you do.

H. J. Harrington

3. Establish a vision and set of values that reflect the desired change behaviors.
4. Establish the recognition and rewards system that supports cultural change behaviors.

Let me end this chapter with just a few thoughts for you to ponder.

Innovation is not creating a new and unique idea. It's knowing what to do with it afterwards.

H. J. Harrington

The right-hand side of the brain is the creative part of the brain that passes ideas on to the left side of the brain. The left-hand side of the brain selects potential innovation ideas for potential implementation.

H. J. Harrington

You don't have innovation unless the idea has value to the external customer and the organization.

H. J. Harrington

Over 95% of our useful ideas are created using continuous improvement methodologies. Less than 5% are innovative.

H. J. Harrington

An organization's CEO who takes his vacation hunting in Africa was talking to the VP. After a lengthy presentation by the VP explaining why his assignment will not be done on time, the CEO stated, "I don't have any room on the wall for additional trophy heads. Which head do you want to replace?"

H. J. Harrington

Section VI

Summary

18

Innovative Change Management Summary

After World War II, we had family-style organizations where management and employees worked together and prospered together. Management and employees both worked for the good of the organization. Then along came the Japanese concept of management and styles changed; teams strived to eliminate waste, and management saw it as the way to eliminate people. Methodologies emerged like reengineering, redesign, Six Sigma, and Lean, which are all directed at cutting costs and jobs, which as a result broke up the "family"-style management. Everyone started to look out for themselves because the organization was only looking out for itself. The cardinal rule of the day became, "Take care of number 1." Play it safe. Don't volunteer for anything, and never suggest anything. Always do exactly what management told you to do. That way you couldn't get into trouble.

> Change is not a matter of luck; it's a matter of design.
>
> **H. J. Harrington**

No matter where you look or where you go (China, Indonesia, India, Argentina, Brazil, South Africa, Egypt, Iraq, etc.), someone (your next-door neighbor in his garage or the woman on the beach in Bali) is trying to design something new and better than what you're doing today. Customers are impressed and looking for the product that has the best design quality, and cost is a second-level consideration. Everything is changing—dresses are getting shorter, dresses are getting longer, pink is the "in" color for fall, the black suit and tie have given way to jeans and T-shirts, and so on. Everything has changed, but most business approaches stalled in the 1960s. Since that date, business design has changed very little and has not kept up with today's needs. What the boss says gets the team to make the decisions that no one can be held accountable for.

People began to live to the old hammer and nail theory: "The nail that sticks up the highest is the first to get hit down."

We are now in the new era moving from knowledge management to innovation management that is requiring the organization to adapt a very different style and objective. With the business environment changing so fast, management must address the problem of how you keep upgrading the skills required to do future work assignments without replacing the management and employees with people who already have those skills and knowledge. What happened to career paths for management and employees? One of the questions I would always ask the new IBM employee was, "What job do you want to retire from 40 years from now?" What happened to employee loyalty? Why is it that most employees look at an assignment with a new organization as a place to hang their hat as they prepare to move on to bigger and better things in another organization?

We don't believe that all changes are designed to build loyalty in our employees. The lack of employee loyalty has had a very detrimental and costly impact on many organizations. Often, each of the negative changes was based on a positive change as viewed by one or more of the stakeholders. Recent improvement initiatives have primarily been based on making the organization more effective (doing more with less). This is exactly what Newton told us would happen, "The third law states that all forces between two objects exist in equal magnitude and opposite direction." It is no surprise that these programs led to a surplus of people as a result of these initiatives. In order to save money, organizations turned the surplus people loose. Cutting back on the workforce supposedly decreased sales prices and increased stockholder and executive compensation. Unfortunately, little or none of the savings were passed on to external customers. With organizations laying off thousands of workers, the workforce quickly realized that management looked at them as an expense, not as an asset. As a result, the workforce changed from having a "family" feel about the organization and loyalty to the organization to a "do what you have to do to get by" attitude. As we look for change, we have to be very cautious in what we implement and how we implement it. For every change, there is a positive and a negative impact on the organization.

I can remember when I was at Ernst & Young and had an office on the tenth floor just across from the coffee machine. The window looked out on the street in front of our building. My office was sandwiched in between two Ernst & Young partners. One sunny April day, a man from our industrial engineering department informed me that in 2 weeks they were going to move my office to the corner office at the end of the building. I really like to work in natural light, and the corner office had over twice as many windows than my present office. I was overjoyed that they were going to move my office, and I was anxious to go home to share the good news with my wife. That night I told my wife the good news, and she immediately asked, "What side of the building is your new office on?" I quickly replied, "Why? It is on the southwest side." She commented, "With all those windows it probably will get awfully hot in the summer. Are you sure you want to move there?" My balloon was busted. Over the next week I went down to the corner office two or three times a day to feel the window, trying to evaluate how hot it would be on a warm summer day in this office. At the end of the first week, I contacted our industrial engineering group and informed them that I didn't want to move out of my present office. He informed me that it was too late as they had already contracted the move and it was going to start in 48 hours. They offered to look for another office when things got settled on. I reluctantly moved into the new office and was pleasantly surprised to see that it had its own thermostat. I was delighted that I could control the temperature. It was a wonderful office, and I was extremely glad that I was lucky enough to get it. Lesson learned: Before you make a change, be sure that you know both the positive and negative impacts that the change will have on you and the organization. Most changes are not as obvious as the move I just presented. Be sure to look down in the darkest, deepest recess to identify the negative things that could impact the stakeholders. The positive things are easy to see. These are the ones that have an impact of a sledgehammer, but the negative ones are as hard to find as a four-leaf clover and are often just as important, or even more important, than the positive changes.

FIFTY WAYS TO IMPROVE

The following are 50 general thoughts about activities that can have a positive impact on innovation and innovative change management (ICM). If you and your team sit down to brainstorm other ideas, you can come up with twice as many ideas that are all directly related to your organization:

1. Conduct area activity analysis
2. Ensure job rotation

3. Provide job descriptions and appraisals for management
4. Give two suggestions per month
5. Revise mission, vision, and values to reflect innovation and trust
6. Consider innovation in evaluating promotions
7. Approve business case
8. Search out people who are dissatisfied, not complaining, but dissatisfied with the job and processes they are involved in and who are committed to improve them
9. Put up posters on CCM
10. Publicize in the organization's newsletter examples of the successful change implementation
11. Improve business case development
12. Lunch with the CEO for the best idea in the function
13. Encourage managers to become angel's advocates instead of devil's advocates
14. Set up opportunity centers to help employees sell their good ideas; help them effectively evaluate and document their ideas
15. Reward the two most creative people each month: one from research and development and one from production
16. Set up development teams that have manufacturing experience
17. Balance development teams with people from manufacturing engineering and quality
18. Hold town meetings
19. Establish synergy in focus groups
20. Install a knowledge management system
21. Identify unofficial leaders in the department, provide them with change agent training and get them involved in the implementation; go out of your way to include some of their suggestions in the implementation plan
22. Provide career planning
23. Award promotions based on training
24. Provide non-work time training paid for by the organization
25. Provide membership to professional societies
26. Improve market studies
27. Give a monthly report to the employees on business-related items
28. Redesign all processes every 3 years
29. Set up a bureaucracy elimination committee
30. Encourage each manager to develop a set of their personal values, keeping it in harmony with the organization's values

31. Literally sell their job to the employees; pay for the work they do
32. Put the internal workers in contact with the external customers (e.g., an assembly worker calls an individual who just bought a product, explaining to the customer that he or she made the product they bought and would like feedback related to it)
33. Encourage open problem-solving—not in a team environment; put a problem on the organization's network so anybody is able to make improvement suggestions related to it
34. Provide feedback to the individual related to the acceptance of his or her product
35. Use the employees as external customers of new products
36. Establish a no-layoff policy
37. Have the employees set targets that management signs off on
38. Rearrange the office
39. Set up think areas within the individual departments
40. Adopt an open-door policy
41. Establish an internal education and learning curriculum
42. Establish a get out of jail free card
43. Help management improve follow-up on assignments
44. Make every manager a change agent
45. Rotate managers every 3 years
46. Ensure all project managers become certified change agents
47. Hire people whose personal values are in line with the organizational values, rather than technology people; you can always train the technology, but it is hard to change someone's personality
48. Plan more family activities
49. Replace managers who are not trusted by their employees, after they've had an opportunity to correct their behaviors; if they don't make the required changes, they should be reassigned to a technical job; you can locate these individuals through the employee opinion survey
50. All too many of our managers and employees act like they are robots; they blindly follow processes that they are programmed to exercise; these humanoids are excellent candidates for the placement

These are just some of the ways that an organization can organize to be more culturally change oriented. I'm sure you can generate a dozen more ideas that would be particularly useful in your environment. The objective of CCM is to develop your employee's emotions so that their negative emotional level will be less severe and the duration of the negative drop is much shorter. When this is accomplished, the resistance to change will almost be eliminated, and the organization will be extremely resilient and supportive of change.

TECHNOLOGIES' IMPACT ON CHANGE

For those of you who are "techies," you probably noticed that I have stayed away from technology's impact on the way the organization needs to change over the next 5 years. This is not something I did by accident, but something that I specifically decided to save for the last due to its importance. In order to adequately address technology's impact (past, present, and future) on your organization, it would require a separate book be devoted to it. It is one of the items that I have added to my list of things to do, and it was a priority item.

Here is one personal example of the impact current technology is having on each of us. Frequently, I go to lunch with a friend who brings three to four cellphones in order to keep him in touch with the rest of the world. (Confidentially, I don't believe he has three or four friends who want to talk with him, let alone can't wait until the normal business day to carry on the same conversation.) This just highlights how we have turned into a "world of instants"—instant phone messages, instant conferences, instant news, instant research, and so on. Why should we think when a computer can do it for us much better than we can ever do it by ourselves? You want a girlfriend, so you go to a dating website and instantaneously your computer gives you the selection between 25 different ladies who match your requirements.

It will not be long and the family doctor will be in a computer. After all, the computer can say, "Take 3 aspirins, drink lots of water, and go to bed. If you're not feeling better in 3 days, let me know." All kidding aside, a computer can check your vital measurements and give you medical advice without you ever leaving your home. Some data indicate that a computer can do a much more accurate job of handling patients with initial calls than the doctors can. Self-driving automobiles are already here, and who can forget when identity theft and firewalls were figments of someone's imagination.

Talking is becoming obsolete; it seems for some the standard practice is now texting another individual who is sitting in the same room. None of us could exist without the ever so valuable TV remote control, which allows us to instantaneously switch channels without moving out of our chair. After all, who has the energy to get up and walk 10 feet to the TV just to change the channel? Evolution will cause some major changes in the physical makeup of the humanoids. There will be no need for arms and legs. We will just have a big round body with plenty of padding when it comes in contact with the chair. It will be a three-dimensional video screen allowing us to instantaneously change a lot to meet the individual conditions. The majority of our time will be spent maintaining and repairing our robots, because we will be completely dependent on them. Let's hope it does not go that far, and we can keep technology as an enabler rather than a driver.

> IT is an enabler, not the answer.
>
> **H. J. Harrington**

TECHNOLOGY ON THE MOVE

Technology in change is like bread and butter, apple pie and ice cream, and mashed potatoes and gravy. A good ICM approach is like salt on your food. It brings out the best flavor. The effective use of technology to handle repetitive, time-consuming activities is essential to reduce costs and cycle time, while improving quality and morale. In the last 20 years, computer technology and its supporting software has transformed our lives in our homes and in our businesses. Who would have ever guessed 40 years ago that computers would be standard fixtures in most homes? Who would have guessed that 3- and 4-year-olds would be using computers as toys? Who would have guessed that we would be dependent on the computer to send and receive mail to a greater degree than we depend on the U.S. Postal Service? When the movie, *2001: A Space Odyssey,* came out, we liked the idea of talking to the computer (HAL) and having it do the work, but thought that it was just science fiction, or at least a long, long way into the future. Well, here I am today writing this by dictating to my computer, and it is typing, punctuating, and checking grammar all without my help. It is now 2017, and technology has become what the science fiction writers wrote about. HAL now can be put on our lap and soon will be able to be carried in our shirt pocket.

> E-business and the Internet mean a business model and a way of managing, not just the application of technology.
>
> **Dr. Armand (Val) Feigenbaum**

Yes, technology has collapsed the world into local neighborhoods. I've been involved in projects where we designed the product on the East Coast of the United States, sent the specifications to India electronically to do the programming, and within the same day sent the programs to our simulation laboratory in London. Then London performed the required testing and transmitted the test results back to the design team so that they could work with completed results 16 hours after they prepared the design concept. That's a single 24-hour cycle from the design to test the output with no overtime and no second- and third-shift operations.

> It could take up to three weeks to get all the information about a taxpayer. Now, the automated environment allows this to be done in about 50 seconds.
>
> **Andre Van Der Post**
> *Manager of Innovation, South African Revenue Service*

Technology has also broken down the walls that surround the office by allowing employees to work out of their homes, saving travel time and reducing the costs of expensive office space. For example, when Ernst & Young in San Jose, California, made the move to the home office concept, they were able to reduce their office space by over 50%. The basic concern that many managers have with the home office concept is that they have no control over how the employee is spending his or her time. They question whether the employee is home working or playing with the children or out buying groceries. The real question is, "Does it make any difference when the employee does the company's work?" The answer is no. If it is best for the employee to do his or her work starting at 9 pm after the house has quieted down, he/she should have that option. Management needs to measure results, not the time of the day that the individual employee is working to accomplish those results. As long as the employees complete their assigned tasks on time, within budget, and produce a high-quality output, it shouldn't matter what days of the week or what hours of the day they work. But for you managers who do not trust your employees, there is software that tracks what each employee accomplishes during each hour of the day. This allows complete accountability even in this virtual working environment. A typical software product that accomplishes this is sold by Virtual Enterprise Solutions, located in San Jose, California.

It wasn't long ago that barcode was state-of-the-art, but that technology is fast being made obsolete with Radio Frequency Identification (RFID) and Collaborative Compliance Services (CCS). This is the same technology that is now used by Exxon Mobil Speedpass and E-Z Pass. Imagine going into Safeway, removing a can of Campbell's chicken noodle soup from the shelf, and putting it into your shopping cart. With this simple act, an electronic scanner automatically checks out the products and the cost has been removed from your debit card. In the background, a radio signal notified the stockroom that one can was removed from the shelf, and Campbell's has been notified that one can of Campbell's chicken noodle soup has been sold by that specific Safeway. When sufficient quantities of the product have been sold, as specified by the customer, Campbell's automatically delivers a replacement supply. This is all possible today with RFID. For example, in 2005 Wal-Mart began to require that all of their major suppliers convert to RFID labeling on the products delivered to Wal-Mart. By 2006 they required that all of their other suppliers convert over also. This result is millions of dollars in savings for Wal-Mart and their suppliers through better inventory management, reduced workloads, and reduced pilfering. In addition to these advantages, it improves customer satisfaction by eliminating those long checkout waiting lines. It is estimated that Wal-Mart will save $8.35 billion a year as a result of using RFID. Most of the savings results from reduced labor cost from not having to scan the barcodes of incoming goods. This will also help Wal-Mart solve two of their major problems—out-of-stock items and products lost as a result of theft (shrinkage).

Larry Kellam, Director of Supply-Network Innovation at P&G, stated, "Reducing out-of-stock products by 10%–20% could boost its annual sales by anywhere from $400 million to $1.2 billion." (Source: Fortune Magazine, November 10, 2003.)

Technology Movers

We can go on and on talking about the many different ways technology and software have changed and will be changing our business profiles. Typical technology tools are as follows:

- Customer relations management
- Project portfolio management
- Simulation modeling
- Data warehouse
- Business to business

- Business to customer
- Manufacturing resource(s) planning
- Knowledge management software
- Portals
- Websites
- Distant learning
- Automated testing
- Automated production
- E-Commerce
- Database management systems
- Systems, applications, and products in data processing
- RFID

We discovered that ROI was so high because companies have begun to scope out very specific goals and purchase only those applications that helped the companies do what they wanted to do.

Mary Wardley
VP, IDC
CRM Applications Research

A recent International Data Corporation study of CRM implementations revealed that returns ranged from 16% to 1000%. The IDC study revealed that only 7% of the return was technology related, with 93% the result of understanding the process before information technology was applied.

These technologies have penetrated almost every facet of the excellent organization's business. Sometimes I question if it is all worth the additional costs and bother. The technology is outpacing the employee's ability to implement and make use of it. Theoretically, it all sounds extremely good, but practically, it often outruns the organization's ability to effectively change the culture and get the required employee buy-in. But, if your competitors are using all this modern-day technology and if you do not follow, or better still, lead the trend, you are giving your competitors a significant advantage.

Technology Examples

Microsoft reported the following typical savings from the use of some of their software products:

- Saks Inc. saved over $1 million in payroll and increased productivity by 40%, while decreasing response time from 45 to 8 seconds.
- E-College installed a contact server and call-center solution realizing an annual return on investment (ROI) of 1700%.

The South African Revenue Service (SARS) fixed its fragmented taxpayer information database by installing Siebel Public Sector Single View of the Taxpayer Solution. This provided them with a completely integrated multiple-taxpayer system that generated the following results:

- It paid for itself within 2 months.
- It saved $12 million per week.
- It allowed for more accurate tax assessments, fewer data entry errors, and faster response to inquiries.
- Time to collect taxpayer information was reduced from 3 weeks to 50 seconds.

Overland Storage, a supplier of hardware and software solutions that serviced more than 75,000 customers, had no single repository for call and support information integration. None of the organization's databases were linked together. Superior customer service and support were crucial to the ongoing growth of the organization. As a result, they installed Epicor Software Clientele Customer Support in order to improve customer care, sales support, technical support, internal repair, and quality of software and hardware. The following improvements were measured:

- ROI of 278% in 1 year
- Inventory reduction of 28%
- 5%–15% improvement in customer satisfaction
- 16% improvement in first-time fixes
- 9% improvement in contract renewals

The *Reader's Digest* customer service website was growing fast in usage. The work was handled by an outside supplier. In order to answer the questions, as many as 20 different databases needed to be searched. It was taking too long to respond to its inquiries, and the quality of some of the answers was questionable. They installed Right Now Smart Assistant, which provided *Reader's Digest* with an integrated self-service knowledge base. It even scanned incoming e-mail inquiries and suggested answers. As a result, *Reader's Digest* saw the following improvements:

- 35% improvement in agent productivity
- 35% reduction in processing time
- 360° view of their customers and their history

United Asset Coverage (UAC) streamlined their customer service and sales representative's processes and installed Oracle E-Business. The results were as follows:

- 205% first-year ROI
- $3.4 million recovered annually in savings and revenue
- Invoice cycle time reduced from 1 week to 2 days
- Billing questions now answered in one call

EMI Industries focused on streamlining their customer communications and installed Siebel e-Business Applications. The results were as follows:

- 25% savings in verifying delivery information
- 10% reduction in overtime
- 10% reduction in inventory
- 75% resolution rate on the first call
- 90% time savings to resolve accounts receivable inquiries

IQ Net Solutions focused on its customer relations processes. It streamlined these processes and installed Microsoft CRM. The results were incredible:

- 234% ROI within 5 months
- Much greater commitment servicing customer needs

How Much Should We Rely on Technology?

Technology is not a magic bullet – if you fire technology at poorly constructed sales, marketing or service processes, you will only end up doing inefficient and ineffective activities faster than ever before. Successful CRM often requires some serious process redesign.

Jim Dickie
Partner
CSO Insights

Robert Cole, professor at the University of California at Berkeley, conducted an extensive study on how Japan and the United States were using technology like enterprise resource planning (ERP) and CRM. He reported that the United States was using ERP and CRM 500% more than Japanese organizations. Few of the Japanese organizations were using CRM and ERP, while these software packages were used extensively throughout the United States. He believes that the reason for the difference was that there was a low measurable ROI from ERP and CRM, causing Japanese organizations to not incorporate these software packages, while U.S. organizations justified implementing these packages based on both direct and indirect benefits that they received.

Cole also reported that only 11% of the Japanese organizations had full-time chief information officers (CIOs), while 56% of the U.S. organizations had full-time CIOs. He also reported a vast difference in IT department participation in strategic planning. In the United States, 51% of the organizations included IT, while only 14% of the Japanese organizations included them.

There is no doubt in our minds that IT must play an important role in improving the processes within an organization. But remember, it is just one of the many tools that are available to you. Your best approach to process improvement is simplification. Then, and only then, should you bring in IT to do the repetitive jobs.

PITFALLS TO SUCCESSFUL ICM

Progress is a nice word. But change is its motivator and change has its enemies.

Robert Kennedy
U.S. Senator

A very good friend of ours, Robert P. Reid, in his lectures, covers 14 pitfalls to change management and their related action plan. We feel they are worthwhile repeating here:

- Pitfall 1—No perceived need for change
  - Most individuals and organizations who have a need for change fail to perceive it. Living in denial, individuals and organizations

will accept the status quo until they disappear. For an individual or organization to perceive the need for change, a precipitating event is frequently required.

- Pitfall 2—No support from key individuals
  - For any individual or organization to be successful, they must have support. Support must cover a wide range of time event horizons, address key interactions, and follow visible vectors. You cannot change an organization by yourself. You need a sponsor or a mentor who is higher than you in the organizational structure. You need to form a coalition of supporters to provide the resources necessary to drive the change.
- Pitfall 3—Not focused on the correct goal
  - Focusing on the correct goal by following the visible vector and making it an integral part of any individual or organization is a very difficult thing to do. Much has been published about how to focus on your long-term outlook, focus on your short-term outlook, maintain your status quo, and so forth. Each of these is a good focus at the appropriate time based on your context. Setting the goal and not reviewing it frequently in relation to other interactions of key factors is a recipe for disaster. Any goal must be frequently reviewed and revised and must not become a meaningless mantra to be repeated and used as an obstacle by organizational sludge.
- Pitfall 4—Lack of comprehension of appropriate time event horizon
  - Failure to understand the need to examine interactions in relation to all of the time event horizons leads to less than optimum success. Lack of understanding of the concept of time event horizons causes individuals and organizations to focus on inappropriate change and is a success inhibitor.
- Pitfall 5—Inability to change the status quo
  - Individuals and organizations tend to follow the law of physics that states, "An object at rest tends to stay at rest." Stagnation is a consistent success killer. Most individuals and organizations do not even realize how stagnant they have become. They believe that because they have come out with a new product, rearranged their physical surroundings, or reorganized their reporting structure, they have made progress. Many find it easier to do nothing or make minor cosmetic changes than to meaningfully address what it takes to influence the major interactions of the

status quo. Organizational sludge fights unmercifully to maintain the current bureaucracy and methods.

- Pitfall 6—No way to keep score
  - Individuals and organizations tend to follow the law of physics that without a way to measure progress, it is impossible to determine if anything is actually being done. Frequently, individuals and organizations have no understanding of what is truly being measured, the value of the measurements, and what interactions are actually causing the measurements.
- Pitfall 7—Bubble down
  - Bubble down occurs when an individual or organization starts to focus on a level of change higher than the one they are actually working on. An organization may begin by espousing transformational change but actually work on design, incremental, or no change.Individuals and organizations are undergoing significant and traumatic emotional events as a result of the bubble down phenomenon. A common result is an inordinate amount of focus on profit in organizations and a lowering of the standard of living for those involved with tasks. Focusing on one level and performing at a lower level causes great confusion for those involved in the process and those who are exposed to it. Understanding the relationships of interactions is the key to design or transformational changes, not actions that are taken.
- Pitfall 8—Cognitive dissonance
  - Cognitive dissonance is one of the results of the bubble down model. Cognitive dissonance is the result of saying one thing and doing another. This not only occurs at the high level of transformation and design but also in incremental changes on a daily basis. Those at the top of the organization focus on the visible vector and rarely need or desire to understand how implementation actually occurs. Unfortunately, these changes are usually delegated to the organizational sludge that has little or no incentive to see them succeed. Therefore, the implementation does not resemble what has been stated.
  - Cognitive dissonance frequently occurs when teaming, empowerment, and reengineering are introduced into organizations. It is rare that these types of changes are implemented with any resemblance to what is actually said to those involved.

- At the individual level, we run into cognitive dissonance on a daily basis. Advertisers promise all kinds of benefits for using their products. When we find that some of these benefits are not as great as we expected, we are disappointed or worse. When organizations do something other than what they have said they would do, distrust is fostered.

- Pitfall 9—Copying others
  - Copying the success of others is a path to failure, since their key factors and their interactions are unique to them. Using the ideas of others and integrating them into your own interactions of key factors can produce significant benefits. While this may seem like an obvious statement, few understand it. Benchmarking and competitive analysis have become the way of doing business for many. While imitation may be the most sincere form of flattery, it is not the most effective path to success. It is, in fact, a certain path to failure.

- Pitfall 10—Focusing on only a portion of the process
  - Suboptimization occurs continuously. This pitfall also correlates with pitfall 7, bubble down. It is much easier to focus on only a portion of the equation and call it something else. Efficiency and effectiveness are frequently paired in some form of continuous improvement or total quality management program. Creativity and adaptability through reengineering or system analysis are often considered design change and are seen to improve the chances of success. Context is rarely considered. Although, occasionally, it is the basis for transformation and revolutionary changes.
  - All of these five areas and their interactions form the basis for individual and organizational success. Those striving to follow their path to success must integrate these five areas.

- Pitfall 11—Attempting the impossible
  - Too often, individuals and organizations ignore the key factors and their interactions, which preclude their success on given actions. Instead, they charge ahead, and when they fail, they place the blame on someone else. Individuals and organizations in our society have lost much of their willingness to accept responsibilities for their own actions.
  - To be successful, individuals and organizations must understand what is impossible within their context and not waste effort and

resources attempting to accomplish things that are impossible within their context.

- Pitfall 12—Lack of focus
  - Some of the symptoms of a lack of focus are false starts, over-adjusting, starting over, focusing on past successes, and too many hands on the steering wheel. Many failures can be directly linked to a lack of focus. Individuals and organizations often find it is easier to start something than to finish it. Many of the conglomerates of the recent past have been broken back into their component parts to enable them to have a consistent focus on their marketplace.
  - It takes a great deal of effort to understand the key factors and their interactions. When they are understood, it is possible to maintain a specific focus. It is not appropriate to continuously change focus. The visible vector to be followed should address the issues of the longest meaningful time event horizon. It should be reviewed on a regular basis and be the foundation for change.
- Pitfall 13—Lack of will
  - Successful individuals generate a will to follow. They also have a great will to succeed and are willing to attempt the impossible at appropriate times. They are willing to fail in order to succeed later. They are willing to admit their errors and to accept accolades for their accomplishments.
  - Organizations must have the will to explore new directions. They must have the willingness to change what they deliver, how they deliver it, and how they are organized. The lack of will frequently is the result of a lack of focus and not understanding the organization's context. Many organizations begin a program and then it falls by the wayside. This can damage the employee base in ways that are very difficult to reverse. This type of damage prevents the success of future programs.
- Pitfall 14—Lack of ability to withstand adversity
  - Lack of ability to withstand adversity relates to the ability to have things turn out differently than anticipated. This result is perceived by the individual or organization to be adverse to their benefit. As we have said, value only has meaning to individuals. That value has positive or negative perceptions. It is difficult to overcome the negative perceptions when adversity strikes.
  - Individuals and organizations do not willingly kill their cash cow and transform themselves. It takes a thorough understanding of

the appropriate vector and their interactions to their critical factors to be able to accept negative results of taking a significant risk.

> You think you understand the situation, but what you don't understand is that the situation has changed.
>
> *Putnam Investment Advertisement*

THE TEN COMMANDMENTS OF ICM

The following is what we classify as the 10 Commandments of ICM:

1. Analyze the organization and the need for change.
2. Create a shared vision and common direction.
3. Separate from the past.
4. Create a sense of urgency.
5. Support strong leader roles.
6. Line up political sponsorship.
7. Craft and implement a plan.
8. Develop enabling structures.
9. Communicate, involve people, and be honest.
10. Reinforce and institutionalize change.

MAJOR REFERENCE BOOKS

The following are some of the major reference books the author used in preparing this book:

- *Resource Management Excellence*—H. James Harrington (Paton Press 2007)
- *Permanent Innovation*—Langdon Morris (Innovation Academy 2011)
- *Change Management Excellence*—H. James Harrington (Paton Press 2016)
- *Change Management—Manage the Change or It Will Manage You*—Frank Voehl and H. James Harrington
- *Project Change Management—Applying Change Management to Improvement Projects*—H. James Harrington, Daryl R. Conner, Nicholas L. Horney (McGraw-Hill 2000)

- *Project Management Excellence*—H. James Harrington and Thomas McNellis (Paton Press 2006)
- *Total Improvement Management—The Next Generation in Performance Improvement*—H. James Harrington and James S. Harrington (McGraw-Hill 1995)

RESILIENCE

Definition

Resilience is the ability to absorb high levels of disruptive change while displaying minimal dysfunctional behaviors.
The five characteristics of resilience are as follows:

- Positive—A positive attitude and spirit are normal behavior for employees and management.
- Focus—Everyone understands the importance of his or her assignment and keeps it as the primary focus of his or her activities.
- Flexible—The employees realize that the organization has to continuously transform itself in order to meet customer/consumer requirements. As a result, they are willing to make a 180° shift if it is for the good of the organization.
- Organized—The employees.
- Proactive—Recognizes the opportunity and takes advantage of it. He or she doesn't want to be told what to do. By the time the manager gets around to telling the employee about an opportunity, the employee is already taking advantage of it.

The more resilient your organization's employees are, the greater is the speed of change. It should be the objective of every innovative organization to be technologically advanced and to have resilient people who can recover quickly from changes. Resilient people show the following characteristics:

- Quickly regain their equilibrium after expectations are disrupted
- Maintain a high level of productivity during periods of ambiguity
- Remain physically and emotionally healthy while struggling with uncertainties
- Rebound from the demands of change even stronger than before.

Appendix A

ACRONYMS/GLOSSARY

AAA   Area activity analysis
CCM   Culture change management
ICM   Innovative change management
PM   Project management
PCM   Project change management
TQM   Total quality management

- **Five major innovation areas** that are used in most projects:
  - Management
  - Products
  - Processes
  - Marketing and sales
  - Support services
- **10Ss model:** It is a combination of McKinsey's 7Ss model plus three additional key innovation drivers added by the author. Each cultural driver must be considered when an organization or part of the organization is considering a major change or a high-risk change. Even with low-risk, minor changes these 10 key innovation drivers should be considered in developing the implementation plan although specific emphasis may not be required in many cases.
- **Assimilation stress:** It is the stress put on an individual or organization whenever a change is made either negative or positive. It is the stress that is required to overcome the status quo. Any one point in time, the total assimilation stress is the accumulated stress of all of the individual assimilation stresses. The stress factor you experience is a combination of personal stress (divorce, moving, having a baby, etc.) plus stress related to the work environment and potential new project.

- **Black hole**: A condition where one or more managers fails to fulfill his or her sponsor responsibilities, such as by withholding or distorting information so that it does not get distributed to the rest of the organization.
- **Business case:** A document that captures the reasoning for initiating any project or program. It is most often presented in a well-structured written document, but, in some cases, also may come in the form of a short verbal agreement or presentation. The logic behind the business case is that whatever resources, such as money or effort that will be consumed by the project/activity, should be in support of a specific business need or opportunity.
- **Change**: This is a perceived departure from what was expected. Change is disruptive when a large gap exists between what happened and what was expected.
- **Consequence management techniques:** Prepared to promptly reward those who facilitate acceptance of the project or express displeasure with those who inhibit it.
- **Continuous improvement**: This is a long-term approach to the way the organization is managed. It is a gradual, never-ending change that is focused on increasing the effectiveness and efficiency of an organization to fulfil its policy and objectives. It is not limited to quality initiatives. Improvement in business strategy; innovation; business results; and customer, employee, and supplier relationships can be subject to continual improvement. Put simply, it means "getting better all the time." It includes individual methodologies like reengineering, redesign, and lean, plus a number of other improvement programs like customer relations management software in sales departments and supply chain management in production control.
- **Core capabilities:** The business processes that visibly provide value to the customer (e.g., Honda's dealer management processes).
- **Core competencies:** The technologies and production skills that underlie an organization's products or services (e.g., Sony's skill at miniaturization).
- **Critical success factors:** These are the key things that the organization must do exceptionally well to overcome today's problems and the roadblocks to meeting the vision statement. In short—things that must go right in order to succeed.

- **Cultural assessments:** The primary drivers that help define the cultural improvement tools that should be included in your CCM plan. The three assessments that were conducted in Phase I provide a good road map for a team made up of executives, union officers, and employees. These should be used to construct the CCM plan and to gain buy-in for the plan from the various levels within the organization.
- **Culture:** The beliefs, behaviors, and assumptions shared by individuals within the organization, which include such things as procedures, values, and unspoken norms.
- **Culture change management (CCM):** This focuses on the human side of change as it affects the employees in their day-to-day work activities by creating a resilient culture. CCM emphasizes that the people who make the change happen (or not, in some cases), and their ability to adapt, absorb, and assimilate new ways of operating, ultimately define success. It is a methodology that is designed to minimize the negative impact of social, organizational, process, or product changes on the total organization or a specific function within the organization. It focuses on the culture of the organization rather than on the individual project.
- **Direct stimulation:** This normally takes the form of financial compensation or activities that are related to financial compensation, like salary increases, paid-for trips, paid-for education, and technical conferences.
- **Dysfunctional:** Any change-related activity or feeling that diverts resources away from meeting productivity and quality standards.
- **Frame of reference (FOR):** A compatible set of ideas, theories, beliefs, feelings, values, and assumptions that are applied to a person's experience. The frame of reference is an unconscious model comprehending reality.
- **Functions:** The major parts of the organization that are usually considered as the smokestack of the organization. For example, finance, quality assurance, manufacturing engineering, manufacturing, research and development, human factors, and so on.
- **Future shock:** The point at which people can no longer assimilate change without displaying dysfunctional behaviors.
- **Habits:** Protectable behavior patterns that have been repeated over and over again until they happen automatically without thought

or preplanning. Habits are formed over a long period of time for a series of favorable results as viewed from the individual's standpoint that occurred as a result of an action he or she has taken. Developing favorable habits is one of the primary objectives of the CCM methodology.

- **Indirect stimulation:** This act normally takes the form of nonfinancial recognition. It benefits the organization by instilling pride and degree of satisfaction in the individual. (Typical examples include to increase your office size, to be given the new office by a window, to be awarded trophies or plaques, to be given a new computer, etc.)

- **Initiating sponsor:** The person or group with the power and resources to start the change process.

- **Innovation:** Innovation is a new/unique idea or concept that adds value to the organization and its customers. Innovation is the act of taking unique and creative idea that are developed, funded, produced, and distributed to external customers that result in creating value to both the organization and the consumer/customer.

- **Innovative change management (ICM):** A disciplined framework for driving business results by changing behaviors. It entails managing the effect of new business processes, changes in organizational structure, or cultural changes within an enterprise. The challenge is to apply effective practices to anticipate and minimize resistance to change. It is the combination of PCM and CCM.

- **Monitoring plans:** The determination to ensure that monitoring procedures are established that will track both the transition's progress and problems.

- **Natural work team:** Made up of a manager at any level and all the employees who report directly to him or her. It could be the president and all the vice presidents and support staff that report directly to him or her. It can be the maintenance department manager and all the employees that report directly to him or her.

- **Organization:** Company, corporation, firm, enterprise, or association or any part thereof, whether incorporated or not, public or private, that has its own function and administration (source ISO 8402:1994).

- **Pain:** A level of discomfort with the status quo that makes change attractive.

- **Persistence:** The capacity to demonstrate consistent support for the project and reject any short-term action that is inconsistent with long-term project goals.
- **Personality:** The way an individual and organization react to other individuals and organizations. This outward behavior is based on how the individual and organization believe will meet the individual and/or organization's needs related to their interfaces. Personality will vary to meet the different environments that the individual and organization presently encounter in day-to-day activities. Rapid changes in behavioral patterns usually are a change in personality, not in culture.
- **Power:** The organizational power to legitimize the change with those individuals (targets) whose behavior must change as a result of the project.
- **Private role:** The ability and willingness to meet privately with key individuals or groups to convey strong personal support for the project.
- **Project change management (PCM):** The application of change management methodologies to an individual project to increase its probability of being successful. It is a methodology used to minimize the social, organizational, process, or product changes that could impact the successful implementation of a specific project or program. It does not include job changes to the specific project or program.
- **Project management:** The application of knowledge, skills, tools, and techniques to project activities to meet project requirements. Project management is accomplished through the following:
  - Application and integration of project management
  - Processes of initiating, planning, executing, monitoring, controlling, and closing
- **Public role:** The ability and willingness to demonstrate the public support necessary to convey strong organizational commitment to the project.
- **Resilience:** The ability to absorb high levels of disruptive change while displaying minimal dysfunctional behavior. The five characteristics of resilience are positive, focused, proactive, organized, and flexible.

- **Resources:** A thorough understanding of the organizational resources (e.g., time, money, and people) necessary for a successful project implementation and the ability and willingness to commit them.
- **Risk area:** Any class of activity or lack of activity that reduces the probability of successful project implementation. Examples include resistance, change knowledge, project overload, and implementation skills and techniques.
- **Scope:** The capacity to understand thoroughly the size of the group to be affected by the project.
- **Sensitivity:** The capacity to fully appreciate and empathize with the personal issues that major change raises.
- **Stakeholder:** An individual or group of individuals or organizations with a common interest. Stakeholders of an organization typically are the customers, owners, employees, employees' families, suppliers, and consumers.
- **Sustaining sponsors:** They use their logistics, the economic or political proximity to assist the targets (the individual or group affected by the change), to ensure that the initiating sponsor's directions are implemented.
- **The long view:** A total, in-depth understanding of the effect the project will have on the organization.
- **Value proposition:** A document that provides an early stage estimate of the net benefits that will result from the implementation of a change or the use of an output by one or more of the organization's stakeholders. A value proposition can apply to an entire organization, parts thereof, customer accounts, products, services, or internal processes.
- **Vision:** A clear definition of what change must occur.
- **Willingness to sacrifice:** The commitment to pursue the transition, knowing that a price will most often accompany the project.

Appendix B

LIST OF THE MOST USED AND MOST EFFECTIVE INNOVATIVE TOOLS AND METHODOLOGIES IN ALPHABETICAL ORDER

TABLE B.1

Usage Classification for the Primary Innovative Tools and Methodologies

	Innovative Tools and Methodologies	**Book I**	**Book II**	**Book III**
1.	5 Why questions	S	P	S
2.	76 standard solutions	P	S	
3.	Absence thinking	P		
4.	Affinity diagram	S	P	S
5.	Agile innovation	S		P
6.	Attribute listing	S	P	
7.	Benchmarking		S	P
8.	Biomimicry	P	S	
9.	Brain-writing 6-3-5-	S	P	S
10.	Business case development		S	P
11.	Business plan	S	S	P
12.	Cause-and-effect diagrams		P	S
13.	Combination methods	P	S	
14.	Comparative analysis	S	S	P
15.	Competitive analysis	S	S	P
16.	Competitive shopping		S	P
17.	Concept tree (concept map)	P	S	
18.	Concurrent engineering	P		
19.	Consumer co-creation	P		
20.	Contingency planning		S	P
21.	Co-star	S	S	P
22.	Costs analysis	S	S	P
23.	Creative problem-solving model	S	P	

(Continued)

253

TABLE B.1 (*Continued*)

Usage Classification for the Primary Innovative Tools and Methodologies

	Innovative Tools and Methodologies	Book I	Book II	Book III
24.	Creative thinking	P	S	
25.	Design for tools		P	
	Subtotal number of points	8	7	10
26.	Directed/focused/structure innovation	P	S	
27.	Elevator speech	P	S	S
28.	Ethnography	P		
29.	Financial reporting	S	S	P
30.	Flowcharting		P	S
31.	Focus groups	S	S	P
32.	Force field analysis	S	P	
33.	Generic creativity tools	P	S	
34.	HU diagrams	P		
35.	I-TRIZ	P		
36.	Identifying and engaging stakeholders	S	S	P
37.	Imaginary brainstorming	P	S	S
38.	Innovation blueprint	P		S
39.	Innovation master plan	S	S	P
40.	Kano analysis	S	P	S
41.	Knowledge management systems	S	S	P
42.	Lead user analysis	P	S	
43.	Lotus blossom	P	S	
44.	Market research and surveys	S		P
45.	Matrix diagram	P	S	
46.	Mind mapping	P	S	S
47.	Nominal group technique	S	P	
48.	Online innovation platforms	P	S	S
49.	Open innovation	P	S	S
50.	Organizational change management	S	S	P
51.	Outcome driven innovation	P		
	Subtotal number of points	15	4	7
52.	Plan-do-check-act	S	P	
53.	Potential investor present	S		P
54.	Project management	S	S	P

(*Continued*)

TABLE B.1 (*Continued*)

Usage Classification for the Primary Innovative Tools and Methodologies

	Innovative Tools and Methodologies	Book I	Book II	Book III
55.	Proof of concepts	P	S	
56.	Quickscore creativity test	P		
57.	Reengineering/redesign		P	
58.	Reverse engineering	S	P	
59.	Robust design	S	P	
60.	S-Curve model		S	P
61.	Safeguarding intellectual properties			P
62.	Scamper	S	P	
63.	Scenario analysis	P	S	
64.	Simulations	S	P	S
65.	Six thinking hats	S	P	S
66.	Social networks	S	P	
67.	Solution analysis diagrams	S	P	
68.	Statistical analysis	S	P	S
69.	Storyboarding	P	S	
70.	Systems thinking	S	S	P
71.	Supply chain management	S	P	
72.	Synetics	P		
73.	Tree diagram	S	P	S
74.	TRIZ	P	S	
75.	Value analysis	S	P	S
76.	Value propositions		S	P
77.	Visioning	S	S	P
	Subtotal—number of points	6	13	7

Notes: Book I—Organizational and/or Operational Innovation Tools and Methodologies; Book II—Evolutional and/or Improvement Innovation Tools and Methodologies; Book III—Creative Innovation Tools and Methodologies.

IT&M, innovative tools and methodologies; P, primary usage; S, secondary usage; Blank, Not used or little used.

(P) Priority Rating	Creative	Evolutionary	Organizational
Total	29	24	24

IT&M in Creativity Book	29
IT&M in Evolutionary Book	24
IT&M in Organizational Book	24

Appendix C

MIND EXPANDERS

- The 2-minute mind
- Mindbeats
- The alphabet
- The numbers
- A nursery rhyme
- Common objects
- Personal creativity
- Analyzing outrageous ideas
- Pictures to drive creativity
- Words to drive creativity
- Differences and similarities
- Defining other applications
- Creative progress reports
- Dreaming in colors
- Recording your evening's activities
- Discarding the boom

Index

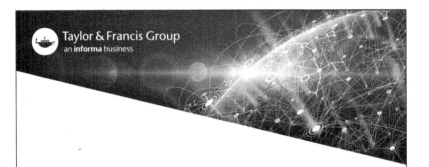